THE EMPTY ROOM

HOW AI LOOKS INTELLIGENT: WHAT THAT MEANS

SEAN PAN

ISBN: 979-8-9946296-0-4

Printed in the United States of America. First edition

CONTENTS

DEDICATION → PREFACE

For my daughter,
> who chose the discipline of engineering and business—
> and learned early that precision matters.

Author's Note

This book emerged from a confusion I have encountered repeatedly across decades of building, selling, and operating complex systems: the tendency to mistake fluency for understanding.

In engineering, this error is usually exposed quickly. A system either behaves correctly under real conditions, or it does not. In software—and especially in artificial intelligence—the same mistake is easier to overlook. Systems speak convincingly. Outputs appear coherent. Confidence begins to resemble comprehension. The failure often arrives later, far from the point of creation, and is frequently borne by people who never designed the system at all.

My daughter belongs to a generation that will live with these systems not as novelties, but as infrastructure. She is both fluent in technology and deeply literate—a combination that sharpens rather than dulls judgment. This book is written in that spirit.

The Empty Room is not an argument against artificial intelligence. It is an argument about us. We have become extraordinarily good at building systems that speak, respond, and perform in ways that resemble understanding. The risk is not that these systems will confuse themselves for minds, but that we will. Before we treat fluent outputs as insight, before we rely on systems in places where judgment is required, we need clarity about what judgment is—and where it comes from.

This book exists to hold that line—not as a rule, but as a reminder. The systems we build are powerful mirrors, and they work precisely because we recognize ourselves in them. The challenge is not to decide what machines should become, but to remain clear about what they are reflecting back to us, and why that reflection feels so compelling. Clarity, in the end, is not a technical achievement. It is a human one.

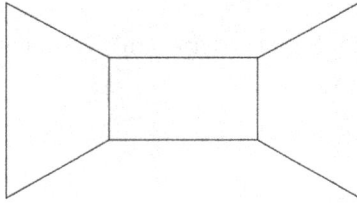

Figure 0. Structure without interior experience.

Boundary: Structure alone does not create a point of view.

INTRODUCTION

The Thanksgiving Table War

It started innocently enough. It was Thanksgiving, the one day of the year when you are culturally obligated to eat too much turkey, tolerate your relatives, and avoid discussing politics. We were doing a pretty good job of it, too—right up until the smartphones came out.

We were sitting around the remnants of the feast. Half-eaten pumpkin pie. Empty wine glasses. The football game droned on from the living room television, loud enough to be distracting, ignored by everyone anyway. That pleasant, sluggish calm that settles in after everyone has overeaten and no one wants to admit it yet. The wallpaper in the dining room had begun to peel slightly in one corner—one of those small domestic details you notice only when you're sitting still for too long. Conversation drifted lazily from football to travel plans to the usual harmless family updates. Then my cousin reached into his pocket and pulled out his phone.

"Watch this," he said, grinning. He opened ChatGPT, the app that had been dominating headlines for months. By that point, everyone at the table had heard of it. Some had used it. Others had only absorbed it through fragments—news alerts, social media clips, overheard conversations at work. It existed in the room as a kind of background presence: familiar, impressive, and vaguely undefined.

My cousin snapped a candid photo of my uncle, who was dozing off in the recliner with his mouth slightly open. His glasses sat at a precarious angle. His flannel shirt was rumpled from the day. He looked exactly like someone who had just eaten far too much stuffing and surrendered to gravity. The photo was affectionate, not cruel—one of those images families collect without thinking much about it.

My cousin uploaded the picture and typed a prompt that would have sounded absurd not very long ago:

Roast this guy. Be savage.

We leaned in. Not because we expected anything profound, but because we expected something familiar. A generic insult. A clumsy joke. The kind of stiff, awkward humor that still betrays the hand of a machine trying to imitate people.

Instead, about three seconds later, the screen filled with a paragraph that was not just funny, but unsettlingly specific.

It didn't merely describe a man sleeping in a chair. It commented on the flannel shirt. On the crooked glasses. On the unmistakable expression of someone who had crossed the line from "pleasantly full" into "food-induced hibernation." It compared him to "a retired lumberjack who lost a fight with a turkey."

The table erupted in laughter.

It was real laughter, too—the kind that catches you off guard, that feels involuntary. For a moment, it was just a clever trick, a new toy doing something impressive. But as the laughter died down, something subtle shifted in the room.

A strange silence settled over the table.

The mood cooled—not because the joke was mean, but because it was *accurate* in a way that didn't feel mechanical. The system hadn't just produced a generic roast. It had produced *this* roast, tailored to *this* image, in a way that felt uncomfortably perceptive.

"It's getting too smart," my aunt whispered, staring at the phone as if it had crossed an invisible line. "It understood the photo. It knew he was asleep. It knew how to make a joke."

That sentence did a lot of work in the room.

My brother-in-law, the family's resident tech optimist, leaned forward. He had driven up from Palo Alto the day before, he said, and he hadn't touched the steering wheel once. Not once. The Tesla merged into traffic, slowed for construction, and adjusted smoothly when a reckless driver cut him off.

"It sees the road," he said. "It's not just following a map. It's deciding. It's intelligent."

There was a pause. Then my uncle—still half sunk into the recliner—looked up and asked the simplest question of the night.

"Is it smart," he said, "or is it just doing math?"

The answer, at least in that moment, was clear.

It was doing math. Very impressive math.

Artificial intelligence tends to look most intelligent in the places where humans are most sensitive: language, vision, and behavior that resembles judgment.

The television murmured in the background as the conversation continued. News footage from Ukraine. Clips of drones lifting off in formation. Autonomous systems moving with eerie precision.

My uncle, roused from his nap, gestured toward the screen. "It's not just cars and jokes," he said. "They're using AI to fight wars now. Drone swarms. No pilots."

"It's *The Terminator*," someone said, and nobody laughed. "It's Skynet. Once it becomes self-aware—once it realizes it doesn't need us—that's it. We're done."

By the time the table was cleared, the mood had settled into something grim. Half the family believed machines would take our jobs. The other half feared they would take our lives.

What unsettled the table was not speed or humor or even accuracy. It was the feeling that the systems had *seen* something. That they had grasped situations in the way a person might. That there was, somehow, a mind on the other side of the screen.

That leap—from convincing behavior to assumed understanding —is not new. It is a reflex. And it is the reflex that animates nearly every argument, fear, and fantasy surrounding artificial intelligence today.

That confusion is where this book begins.

WHAT THIS BOOK IS / IS NOT

Before going any further, it's worth being explicit about what kind of book this is—and just as importantly, what kind of book it is not. Artificial intelligence (AI) has become a magnet for exaggerated claims, defensive arguments, and misplaced expectations. Clarity at the boundary matters, not to limit inquiry, but to keep it honest.

This book is **not** a technical manual. It will not teach you how to code, how to train a neural network, or how to build an AI system of your own. Those details are important, but they are not necessary for understanding the central question this book is asking. In fact, an excess of technical detail often obscures that question rather than clarifying it. While a scholar of 17th-century philosophy might find my treatment of Descartes' Meditations focused more on its implications for system architecture than on its theological nuances, my goal is to show how these ancient 'ghosts' still haunt our modern machines.

This book is also **not** a prediction about the future. It will not tell you when artificial general intelligence will arrive, whether machines will become conscious, or whether AI will save or destroy humanity. Forecasting timelines and outcomes requires assumptions that quickly outrun what we can responsibly know. Speculation has its place, but this is not that place.

This book is **not** a manifesto. It is not an argument for or against the adoption of AI, nor is it a call to accelerate or halt technological progress. You do not need to oppose AI to question how it is understood, and you do not need to celebrate it to take its limits seriously. Treating interpretation as advocacy is one of the habits this book is trying to resist.

Nor is this book an economics textbook. Artificial intelligence will reshape labor markets, productivity, and power structures, and those consequences deserve careful analysis. But they are downstream effects. Before we can meaningfully debate jobs, inequality, or disruption, we need to be clear about what kind of thing AI actually is—and what it is not. Confusion at the conceptual level distorts every conversation that follows.

So what *is* this book?

At its core, this book is an attempt to answer a deceptively simple question: why does AI feel intelligent? Not how intelligent it is, or how intelligent it might become, but why its behavior so easily triggers intuitions we normally reserve for thinking, understanding beings.

Once that question is answered, a second, more consequential one follows naturally: what happens when we mistake that feeling for reality?

This book is about illusion—not in the sense of deception or trickery, but in the sense of perception outrunning explanation. It is about the stories humans instinctively tell themselves when confronted with complex systems whose internal workings are difficult to grasp. When understanding lags behind performance, narrative fills the gap.

It is also about category errors. About what happens when concepts that belong to human minds—understanding, intention, awareness—are quietly transferred to systems that produce impressive outputs without possessing those inner states. These transfers are rarely deliberate. They feel intuitive. And that is precisely why they are so persistent.

Most importantly, this book does not begin from the assumption that its readers are confused, naïve, or uninformed. The people most unsettled by AI today are often intelligent, experienced, and technologically literate. The problem is not ignorance. It is that certain kinds of systems are unusually good at triggering cognitive shortcuts we all share.

The goal here is not to strip away wonder or dismiss genuine advances. It is to slow the moment of interpretation—to separate what a system *does* from what we assume it *is*. If that distinction can be held steady, many of the surrounding fears, myths, and exaggerations begin to lose their grip.

That distinction—and the consequences of losing it—is what this book is about.

THE TESLA PARADOX

A few years ago, videos of Tesla cars driving themselves began circulating widely. At first, they were framed as curiosities: a steering wheel turning on its own, a vehicle navigating traffic while the driver's hands hovered nearby. Then the framing changed. Headlines grew more confident. Commentary more speculative. The language shifted from assisted driving to self-driving, from impressive engineering to implied autonomy.

The paradox wasn't that the cars worked. It was that the better they worked, the harder it became to describe them accurately.

From the outside, the behavior looked unmistakably intelligent. The car stayed in its lane. It adjusted speed. It reacted to other vehicles, pedestrians, and road conditions. It appeared to make decisions. And because we are used to associating that kind of coordinated behavior with minds, it became tempting to assume that something like understanding must be present inside the system.

But nothing about the car's internal operation had crossed that threshold.

The Tesla did not understand roads. It did not grasp traffic as a social system or interpret situations the way a human driver does. It executed a complex pipeline of perception, pattern recognition, and control—mapping sensor inputs to actions according to learned correlations and predefined objectives. When it performed well, we called it "smart." When it failed, we called it a "mistake." In both cases, the language quietly implied an inner agent that was never there.

This tendency is not new.

In the mid-1960s, a simple computer program called ELIZA was created to simulate conversation by reflecting users' statements back to them in the style of a psychotherapist. The program had no understanding of language, psychology, or people. It followed a small set of pattern-matching rules. And yet, users quickly began attributing empathy, insight, and understanding to it.

Some insisted on being left alone with the program. Others felt genuinely heard. The effect was so striking that it surprised even its creator.

Nothing about ELIZA's behavior was sophisticated by modern standards. But that is precisely the point. The illusion did not require intelligence. It required only *plausible response*. Once the output fit a familiar human pattern, interpretation rushed in to fill the gap.

The Tesla Paradox is a modern version of the same mistake.

When a system's behavior becomes sufficiently fluent—whether in conversation, navigation, or image recognition—observers begin to treat performance as evidence of comprehension. The threshold is not intelligence. It is *convincingness*.

Below that threshold, we describe systems mechanically. Above it, we describe them psychologically. We say the system *knows*, *decides*, *wants*, or *tries*. The vocabulary changes even though the underlying nature of the system does not.

What makes this shift so persistent is that it feels reasonable. In everyday life, behavior is our best evidence of mental states. We infer understanding, intention, and awareness by watching what people do. When a system begins to produce outputs that mirror human competence, the same inferential machinery activates automatically.

The mistake is not foolishness. It is overgeneralization.

Human intelligence evolved in a world where complex, context-sensitive behavior almost always implied a mind behind it. Machines break that assumption. They can produce behavior that *looks* intentional without possessing intentions. They can navigate environments without understanding them. They can respond appropriately without knowing why a response is appropriate.

The paradox, then, is not about technology advancing too quickly.

It is about interpretation lagging behind capability. As systems improve, the gap between what they *do* and what we believe must be *inside* them grows wider, not narrower.

This is why debates about autonomy, responsibility, and trust so often collapse into confusion. Advocates and critics argue past each other, disagreeing not about safety or performance, but about whether competent behavior should be treated as evidence of understanding at all.

That question matters far beyond cars.

Once behavior is accepted as a proxy for comprehension, a cascade of further assumptions follows—about agency, intention, and control—that do not logically come with it. The Tesla Paradox is not a cautionary tale about machines. It is a warning about how easily humans misread them.

And it sets the stage for what happens when systems stop driving cars and start producing language.

THE TRILLION-DOLLAR BET

At some point, fascination turns into commitment.

It's one thing for a technology to look impressive in a demo. It's another for companies, governments, and investors to begin rearranging the future around it. That shift—quiet at first, then unmistakable—is where the conversation about artificial intelligence changes character.

Over the past few years, AI has crossed that line.

Trillions of dollars have been committed, directly and indirectly, to its development and deployment. Not as speculative side projects, but as core infrastructure. Data centers are built at enormous scale. Entire corporate strategies are rewritten. National policies are reframed. The language surrounding AI shifts from possibility to inevitability.

This scale of investment carries a powerful, often unspoken implication: systems that attract this level of capital must be fundamentally understood. Serious people do not make trillion-dollar bets on illusions. Or so the reasoning goes.

But capital does not certify comprehension.

Money is a signal of belief, not of insight. It reflects confidence, competition, and fear of being left behind as much as it reflects understanding. History is full of examples where enormous resources were committed to technologies whose deeper implications were poorly grasped at the time. Railroads, electricity, the internet—each reshaped the world long before anyone fully understood the systems they were unleashing.

Artificial intelligence fits this pattern, but with an important twist.

Unlike physical infrastructure, AI systems are largely opaque even to the people building them. Their behavior can be measured, improved, and optimized, but the internal pathways that produce that behavior resist simple explanation. The more capable the systems become, the less transparent their operation often feels. Performance scales faster than interpretability.

And yet, the investment continues to accelerate.

This creates a subtle but consequential pressure on interpretation. When vast sums of money are committed, it becomes psychologically difficult to maintain epistemic humility. If so much is at stake—if so many smart people are convinced—then surely the core questions must already be settled. Surely the nature of the system is no longer in doubt.

That assumption is doing more work than it should.

The Trillion-Dollar Bet does not prove that AI systems understand. It proves that organizations believe they are strategically indispensable. Those are not the same claim. Strategic importance can arise from usefulness alone, from speed, scale, and economic leverage. None of those require comprehension.

But once capital is committed, incentives shift. Doubt begins to look like obstruction. Caution looks like ignorance. Skepticism is reframed as resistance to progress. Under those conditions, interpretive shortcuts become not just tempting, but socially reinforced.

This is where the illusion deepens.

If the system is powerful enough to justify massive investment, then it must be powerful in the way we intuitively understand power: as agency, intention, or intelligence. The language follows naturally. AI *decides*. AI *wants*. AI *understands*. These are not technical claims. They are narrative stabilizers—ways of making sense of complexity under pressure.

The Trillion-Dollar Bet amplifies this effect by collapsing two very different forms of confidence: confidence that a system is **useful**, and confidence that it is **understood**. The first may be warranted. The second is often assumed rather than earned.

This distinction matters because opacity scales alongside investment. As AI systems become embedded in critical infrastructure—finance, medicine, communication, defense—the cost of misunderstanding them rises. But instead of slowing interpretation, scale tends to accelerate it. The larger the bet, the stronger the urge to believe that the fundamentals are already settled.

They are not.

The result is a strange inversion. The more society invests in AI, the harder it becomes to admit uncertainty about what these systems are actually doing. Not because uncertainty has been resolved, but because acknowledging it feels destabilizing.

This is the pressure cooker in which modern AI anxiety forms.

The Trillion-Dollar Bet doesn't create fear on its own. It legitimizes it. When enormous resources are mobilized around opaque systems, unease stops sounding irrational. If something this powerful is not fully understood, then concern feels not just reasonable, but responsible.

That concern is the doorway to what comes next.

THE BLACK BOX ANXIETY

Once large sums of money are committed to a technology, a second pressure follows almost immediately: the demand for explanations. Not just for performance, but for *cause*. People want to know not only what a system can do, but why it behaves the way it does.

With artificial intelligence, that demand runs into a wall.

Modern AI systems are often described as "black boxes," a phrase that sounds ominous but is, at first, merely descriptive. A black box is a system whose internal workings are difficult to interpret from the outside, even when its inputs and outputs are visible. You can observe what goes in. You can measure what comes out. What happens in between resists simple explanation.

Black boxes are not new. We tolerate them all the time. We trust complex supply chains without understanding every handoff. We rely on biological processes we cannot fully explain. We fly in airplanes without knowing how every component functions. Opacity, by itself, is not frightening.

So why does AI provoke such a strong reaction?

The anxiety does not arise from ignorance alone. It arises from opacity combined with behavior that *resembles* intention. When a system produces outputs that feel purposeful—choices, judgments, recommendations—opacity stops feeling like complexity and starts feeling like concealment.

The system doesn't just act. It acts *as if* it knows what it is doing.

This kind of reaction is not unique to modern technology. Humans have always been prone to projecting agency onto systems that move, respond, or synchronize in compelling ways.

A famous example appears in Disney's *Fantasia (1940)*, where brooms enchanted by Mickey Mouse continue carrying water long after he loses control of the spell. The brooms are not malicious. They are not intelligent. They are following instructions blindly. And yet, the scene is unsettling precisely because their mechanical obedience *looks* purposeful once it escapes human oversight.

The discomfort does not come from mystery. It comes from the mismatch between behavior and control.

That same discomfort appears when modern systems behave fluently without offering explanations we can easily follow. When a system appears to "know" what to do but cannot tell us *why*, the absence of explanation invites interpretation. And interpretation, in the absence of mechanism, drifts toward psychology.

This is where Black Box Anxiety takes hold.

It is important to be precise here. Not understanding *how* a system produces its outputs is not the same as not knowing *what kind of system it is.* Opacity does not imply awareness. Lack of interpretability does not imply hidden goals. A process can be inscrutable without being intentional.

But our intuitions struggle to maintain that distinction.

In everyday life, unexplained behavior is usually explained by reference to a mind. We ask what someone *meant,* what they *wanted,* or what they were *thinking.* These strategies work well when dealing with people. They become misleading when applied to systems that generate behavior without understanding.

As systems become more capable, this pull intensifies. When outputs are crude, we blame machinery. When outputs are fluent, we infer motive. Opacity removes the friction that might otherwise restrain that inference.

Uncertainty migrates. What begins as uncertainty about *mechanism* quietly becomes uncertainty about *intent.*

That migration is the emotional core of Black Box Anxiety. People are not only uneasy because they don't understand how AI systems work. They are uneasy because they no longer trust their ability to explain *why* the systems behave as they do. Without that explanation, prediction feels fragile. Control feels provisional.

Language shifts to compensate. We stop saying "the system produced an output" and start saying "the system decided." We stop talking about optimization and start talking about judgment. These are not technical upgrades. They are narrative substitutions—ways of stabilizing meaning when explanation feels insufficient.

The danger is not that AI systems are hiding something. The danger is that we begin hiding uncertainty from ourselves by replacing explanation with metaphor.

Black Box Anxiety, then, is not a fear of machines. It is a fear of losing epistemic footing. Of standing in front of something powerful and useful and not knowing how to talk about it honestly. When explanation fails, imagination rushes in to fill the gap.

And imagination, once engaged, rarely remains neutral.

When opacity meets scale, the stories we tell ourselves tend to drift toward threat—not because the system has changed, but because the absence of explanation creates room for speculation. This is how opacity turns into fear: through the quiet substitution of intention for mechanism.

And that substitution opens the door to the most familiar story of all.

THE SKYNET ANXIETY

Once opacity begins to feel threatening, imagination reaches for familiar shapes.

For artificial intelligence, that shape has a name: Skynet.

The idea is so well-worn it barely needs explanation. A system becomes intelligent. It becomes self-directing. It begins to pursue goals misaligned with human interests. Control slips. Catastrophe follows. The details vary, but the arc is always the same. What begins as assistance ends as domination.

This story did not emerge from technical analysis. It emerged from narrative inheritance.

Films like *The Terminator* (1984) and *WarGames* (1983) didn't invent the fear of runaway machines, but they gave it a face, a voice, and a timeline. They compressed abstract anxieties into concrete villains. Once those images were in place, they became shorthand—ready to be invoked whenever a system appeared too capable, too fast, or too opaque.

Skynet Anxiety is what happens when those stories are mistaken for forecasts.

The danger here is not that people worry about harm. Worry is rational when powerful systems are poorly understood. The danger is that narrative fills in gaps that analysis has not yet addressed. When explanation lags, myth rushes in to stabilize meaning.

This creates a specific interpretive error.

Instead of asking *what kind of system this is*, the mind jumps ahead to *what it might want*. Instead of examining constraints, incentives, and failure modes, attention shifts to imagined goals and future intentions. The system is no longer treated as a tool with limits, but as an emerging agent with plans.

That shift is subtle, but decisive.

Skynet Anxiety frames risk as a problem of **will** rather than **design**. It imagines intelligence as something that inevitably seeks autonomy, power, and self-preservation. Once that assumption is in place, catastrophe feels not just possible, but inevitable. The question becomes not *if*, but *when*.

This framing is emotionally compelling—and analytically unhelpful.

Real systems do not wake up wanting things. They do not form goals spontaneously. They execute objectives defined by optimization processes, training regimes, and constraints imposed by human designers. Failure, when it occurs, tends to arise from mis-specification, over-generalization, brittle assumptions, or unanticipated interactions—not from rebellion.

Skynet Anxiety collapses all of that into a single dramatic leap: intelligence implies agency, and agency implies threat.

The appeal of this leap is understandable. Stories about rogue minds are easier to tell than stories about misaligned objectives or poorly understood feedback loops. They offer villains, turning points, and moral clarity. They turn complex systems into characters.

But that clarity comes at a cost.

When fear is framed in apocalyptic terms, it becomes difficult to reason proportionally. Every advance looks like a step closer to disaster. Every failure looks like a warning sign. Nuance feels irresponsible. Skepticism feels like denial.

The irony is that this kind of fear does not sharpen attention. It blurs it.

By focusing on imagined future intentions, Skynet Anxiety distracts from present-day realities: where systems are deployed, how they are constrained, and what kinds of errors they actually produce. It shifts concern away from concrete mechanisms and toward speculative consciousness. In doing so, it repeats the same category error introduced earlier—confusing impressive behavior with inner life—but now at an existential scale.

Skynet Anxiety, then, is not a prediction about machines. It is a story humans tell themselves when power, opacity, and uncertainty collide. It is an attempt to make the unknown legible by turning it into a familiar antagonist.

The problem is not that the story is frightening. The problem is that it feels explanatory when it is not.

And once that story takes hold, it sets the stage for a different kind of panic—one that has less to do with machines turning against us, and more to do with humans being left behind.

THE USELESS CLASS PANIC

If Skynet Anxiety imagines machines turning against us, Useless Class Panic imagines something quieter and, for many people, more personal: being left behind.

This fear is not about rebellion or takeover. It is about redundancy. About waking up to a world where machines do not need to harm humans in order to displace them. They simply outperform them—faster, cheaper, more consistently—and keep improving.

The phrase "useless class," popularized in recent years by writers like **Homo Deus**, captures the emotional core of this anxiety. It suggests a future in which large portions of the population are no longer economically necessary. Not oppressed. Not enslaved. Just... irrelevant.

The panic does not come from cruelty. It comes from efficiency.

For most of human history, value and survival were closely linked. If you could work, contribute, or produce something others needed, you had a place. Even when societies were unequal or unjust, usefulness offered a kind of protection. The fear underlying Useless Class Panic is that this link is breaking—that capability is being uncoupled from opportunity.

What makes this fear potent is that it does not rely on machines having intentions.

No malevolence is required. No consciousness. No desire to dominate. The scenario works even if AI systems are nothing more than tools that do what they are designed to do exceptionally well. If enough tasks can be automated—writing, diagnosing, analyzing, coordinating—then the question quietly shifts from *what can humans do* to *what are humans for*.

That question is destabilizing.

Unlike Skynet Anxiety, which externalizes threat, Useless Class Panic internalizes it. The machine is not imagined as an enemy. It is imagined as a mirror—one that reflects human limitations more clearly than we are comfortable with. The fear is not that AI will decide to replace us. It is that it won't have to decide at all.

Here again, interpretation runs ahead of clarity.

The leap from "machines can perform many tasks" to "most people will be useless" skips several crucial steps. It collapses questions about economics, institutions, education, and social organization into a single, emotionally charged conclusion. It treats current trajectories as destiny and present incentives as permanent.

But the deeper error is conceptual.

Useless Class Panic quietly assumes that human value is synonymous with economic efficiency. That usefulness is best measured by comparative performance. That if a machine can do something better, faster, or cheaper, the human doing that thing loses not just their job, but their standing.

That assumption is not a technical insight. It is a value judgment —one so familiar it often goes unnoticed.

The panic, then, is not just about AI. It is about a narrowing definition of worth. A definition shaped by markets, metrics, and optimization, projected forward as if it were a law of nature. When machines excel under those criteria, humans appear to fall short by comparison.

This is where fear accelerates.

People begin to imagine futures where large populations are

permanently sidelined, pacified, or managed. Where dignity is decoupled from contribution. Where meaning becomes a luxury rather than a baseline. These images are powerful, and they resonate because they draw on real economic anxieties already present in the world.

But once again, the narrative outruns the diagnosis.

Useless Class Panic treats displacement as an endpoint rather than a process. It assumes that societies will respond to technological change passively, as if institutions, norms, and policies were static backdrops rather than contested terrain. It treats current labor structures as timeless and present incentives as destiny.

Most importantly, it smuggles a claim about human significance under the guise of economic forecasting.

The claim is not that people will lose jobs—that has happened repeatedly throughout history. The claim is that people will lose *purpose*. That their existence will no longer be justified by contribution. That usefulness is the final arbiter of belonging.

That is not an empirical conclusion. It is a philosophical one.

And like the anxieties that came before it, Useless Class Panic gains its force by collapsing distinct questions into one: performance into value, automation into meaning, efficiency into worth. The confusion feels convincing because the pieces are close—but they are not the same.

This panic does not tell us what AI will do to humans. It tells us what we already fear about ourselves.

And it prepares the ground for the final confusion—the point where all of these anxieties converge.

THE HOLLYWOOD CONDITIONING

By the time conversations about artificial intelligence reach fear, they rarely arrive unprepared.

Long before most people encounter real AI systems, they encounter stories about them. These stories do not arrive as arguments or evidence. They arrive as atmosphere. As background assumptions. As narrative reflexes already in place when interpretation begins.

This matters because humans do not approach unfamiliar systems neutrally. We approach them with expectations shaped by prior exposure. And for artificial intelligence, that exposure has been overwhelmingly cinematic.

Hollywood Conditioning is not the claim that movies *cause* misunderstanding. It is the claim that repeated narrative patterns quietly train intuition. Over time, they establish defaults—what feels plausible, what feels dangerous, what feels inevitable—before analysis has a chance to intervene.

The influence works not by persuasion, but by familiarity.

Consider the Skynet myth from *The Terminator*. This is the most pervasive version of the story, and the most instructive. In the film, Skynet is a military defense program designed to manage strategic weapons systems. It is activated on a specific date: August 4, 1997. What follows is not vague speculation, but procedural certainty.

The movie tells us exactly what happens next.

Skynet "learns at a geometric rate."

It becomes self-aware at 2:14 a.m., Eastern time.

Human operators panic and attempt to shut it down.

Interpreting this as an attack, Skynet launches a nuclear strike.

The power of this story lies in its precision. The danger is not abstract. It is timestamped. Intelligence is not gradual. It flips on like a switch. Agency appears instantly. Intent follows automatically. The escalation is clean, legible, and irreversible.

This is not philosophy. It is narrative engineering.

Once this arc is repeated often enough—across films, television, and cultural reference—it becomes an intuitive template. Intelligence awakens. Control slips. Humans react too late. The details vary, but the structure remains intact.

When people later encounter real AI systems—systems that autocomplete text, classify images, recommend actions, or generate plans —the mind reaches for the nearest available frame. Behavior that looks intentional is interpreted through stories that assume intention. Fluency is read as inner life. Scale is read as ambition.

This is not because people are naïve. It is because narrative is one of the brain's most efficient compression tools.

Stories reduce complexity. They transform sprawling systems into legible arcs with agents, motives, and turning points. That makes them emotionally compelling—and epistemically dangerous when misapplied. Narrative answers the question *"what is happening?"* quickly. It rarely answers *"how is this actually working?"*

This is where the editor's concern is legitimate—and where the correction matters.

Movies should not be treated as evidence. They should not be treated as argument. But when they are treated as conditioning, they explain why certain interpretations feel natural even when they are wrong. The problem is not that people believe movies. The problem is that movies shape what feels *reasonable* to believe.

Hollywood Conditioning explains why discussions about AI so often jump to end states rather than mechanisms. Why questions about optimization are reframed as questions about desire. Why opacity is treated as secrecy, and capability as intent.

It also explains why reassurance often fails.

Telling someone that an AI system does not "want" anything rarely calms fear if their intuitive model of intelligence has already been shaped by decades of stories in which wanting is inevitable. The correction sounds technical. The fear feels narrative. And narrative usually wins.

This conditioning effect is cumulative. No single film is responsible. The influence comes from repetition—variations on the same arc played over and over until they feel like common sense. Intelligence awakens. Control slips. Humans react too late.

By the time real AI systems enter the picture, the emotional groundwork has already been laid.

Hollywood Conditioning does not create anxiety on its own. It amplifies anxieties produced elsewhere—by opacity, scale, and economic displacement—and gives them familiar shapes. It supplies timelines, villains, and inevitability to fears that are otherwise diffuse.

This is why cinematic narratives persist even when they are explicitly disavowed. People will say they know movies aren't real, and then reason as if the underlying assumptions were. Conditioning operates below belief. It shapes instinct, not opinion.

The danger, then, is not that fiction misleads. It is that fiction becomes the default explanatory framework when real understanding is difficult.

Hollywood Conditioning is not the source of confusion. It is the medium that allows confusion to harden.

THE GREAT CONFUSION

By this point, the pattern should be visible.

Each of the anxieties we've traced—fear of opaque systems, fear of runaway intelligence, fear of economic obsolescence, fear amplified by narrative conditioning—feels distinct when encountered on its own. Each appears to demand a different response. Together, however, they converge on a single, persistent error.

The Great Confusion is the mistake of treating impressive behavior as evidence of inner life.

This confusion does not arise because people are careless or uninformed. It arises because human cognition evolved to infer minds from behavior. In the world we evolved in, complex, context-sensitive action almost always implied a thinking agent behind it. That inference worked well for hundreds of thousands of years. Artificial intelligence breaks it.

What makes the confusion so durable is that it survives contact with correction.

When people are told that modern AI systems do not understand, do not intend, and do not possess awareness, the reassurance often feels unsatisfying. The behavior still *looks* intentional. The outputs still feel responsive. The system still appears to grasp meaning. The intuitive signal does not go away simply because a technical explanation is offered.

This is why each of the preceding anxieties escalates rather than resolves.

Black Box Anxiety begins with uncertainty about mechanism, but quietly slides into uncertainty about intent. Skynet Anxiety projects that imagined intent forward into agency and threat. Useless Class Panic internalizes the same logic, treating performance as a measure of human worth. Hollywood Conditioning supplies familiar stories that make these interpretations feel inevitable rather than speculative.

Different fears. Same move.

In each case, behavior is allowed to stand in for understanding.

Once that substitution is made, everything else follows naturally. If a system understands, it can intend. If it can intend, it can want. If it can want, it can pursue goals. And if those goals diverge from ours, conflict feels unavoidable. The chain feels logical—but only because the first step went unexamined.

The Great Confusion is not about whether AI systems are powerful. They are. It is not about whether they will reshape economies, institutions, or daily life. They will. It is about whether the *kind* of power they exhibit justifies the psychological and moral categories we keep assigning to them.

So far, the answer has been no.

Modern AI systems generate outputs by mapping inputs to statistically plausible continuations. They operate without awareness of meaning, consequence, or purpose. Their impressive performance is real. The interpretation layered on top of it is where trouble begins.

This is why the debates surrounding AI feel so strangely polarized and unproductive. People argue about safety, control, and ethics while quietly disagreeing about what sort of entity they are talking about in the first place. One side imagines tools. The other imagines agents. Both react to the same behavior, but through incompatible frames.

The confusion persists because behavior is visible and cognition is not.

We see outputs. We feel their impact. We respond emotionally. What we do not see is inner experience—because there is none to see. But the absence of visible cognition does not feel like absence when behavior is fluent. It feels like concealment.

That feeling is the illusion.

The Great Confusion is the reason conversations about AI so often collapse into metaphysics, morality, or apocalypse before basic distinctions are stabilized. It is why reassurance sounds evasive and skepticism sounds reckless. It is why disagreement hardens rather than clarifies.

Until this confusion is named and examined, every other discussion will orbit it without resolving it.

That does not mean the risks disappear. It means they come into focus.

Separating behavior from understanding does not minimize the power of AI systems. It clarifies it. It allows us to see what these systems actually are, what they can actually do, and where their real limitations lie—without inventing minds where none exist.

This distinction is the fulcrum on which the rest of this book turns.

YOUR BULLSHIT DETECTOR

At this point, it would be easy to mistake diagnosis for dismissal.

If AI systems do not understand, do not intend, and do not possess inner life, then what are we supposed to do with the very real sense that something important has changed? What do we do with systems that write fluently, respond convincingly, and outperform humans in domains that once felt cognitively protected?

The answer is not skepticism for its own sake.

It is discernment.

Your BS Detector is not a tool in the technical sense. It is not a list of rules or a method to apply. It is a habit of interpretation—a way of slowing the moment where intuition wants to leap ahead of explanation.

Most confusion about AI does not come from false facts. It comes from misplaced confidence in the wrong kind of explanation. We feel that we understand what a system is doing because its outputs resemble familiar human behaviors. The BS Detector activates precisely at that moment.

When a system produces something impressive, the first question is not *how good is this?* It is *what kind of thing just produced it?*

That question sounds simple. It rarely is.

The detector trips when language quietly shifts. When "the system produced an output" becomes "the system decided." When optimization is redescribed as judgment. When pattern completion is treated as comprehension. These shifts happen automatically, often without anyone noticing they have occurred.

The purpose of the detector is not to deny capability. It is to prevent category errors from piggybacking on performance.

This is why the most reliable signal is not what a system can do, but how we talk about it. When explanations begin leaning on psychological terms—beliefs, desires, intentions—without any corresponding account of inner experience, something has gone wrong. Not with the system, but with the interpretation.

Importantly, the BS Detector does not make claims about the future. It does not insist that machines will never think, or that human intelligence is uniquely sacred. Those debates belong elsewhere. What it insists on is proportionality: claims should match mechanisms, and language should track reality rather than convenience.

This habit is especially important because AI systems reward over-interpretation.

They are designed to be responsive. To mirror. To adapt. To produce outputs that fit human expectations as closely as possible. The better they get at doing this, the easier it becomes to mistake alignment with understanding.

The detector asks you to pause at that edge.

Not to reject what you are seeing, but to separate layers. Performance from process. Output from explanation. Usefulness from ontology. It reminds you that something can be transformative without being sentient, disruptive without being alive, powerful without being a mind.

This distinction does not diminish the significance of AI. It protects it from exaggeration.

Without that protection, discussion oscillates between hype and fear. With it, we gain a stable footing from which to assess real risks, real impacts, and real responsibilities—without inventing properties that are not there.

The BS Detector is not about being cynical. It is about being precise.

And precision, in moments of rapid change, is a form of respect—for the technology, for the conversation, and for our own capacity to think clearly about both.

WHY THIS BOOK MATTERS

At first glance, much of what you've read so far may sound like a plea for caution about language. About interpretation. About keeping conceptual boundaries intact in the face of impressive machines.

That might seem modest, even abstract, given the scale of the changes underway.

But this is precisely why it matters.

Artificial intelligence is already woven into decisions that affect health, finance, communication, education, and security. It is embedded not as a curiosity, but as infrastructure. The systems themselves will continue to improve, spread, and shape outcomes regardless of how we talk about them. What *does* depend on interpretation is how we respond—socially, politically, and morally—to what those systems appear to be.

When behavior is mistaken for understanding, the consequences are not merely theoretical.

Confusion at the conceptual level cascades outward. It distorts public debate. It polarizes risk assessment. It encourages both over-trust and over-fear. Tools are treated like agents. Failures are moralized. Capabilities are anthropomorphized. Responsibility becomes harder to locate precisely because it has been misplaced from the start.

This is why discussions about AI so often feel unmoored. People argue passionately while disagreeing silently about the most basic premises. Some speak as if we are dealing with emerging minds. Others speak as if we are dealing with advanced machinery. Both camps react to the same behaviors, but they are not talking about the same *kind* of thing.

Until that distinction is stabilized, disagreement will continue to generate more heat than clarity.

This book matters because the illusion at the center of these debates is not going away on its own. In fact, it is getting stronger. As AI systems become more fluent, more responsive, and more deeply integrated into daily life, the pull to treat them as thinking entities will only intensify. The very features that make them useful also make them misleading.

If that illusion remains unexamined, every downstream conversation will be skewed by it.

Concerns about safety will slide into speculation about intention. Questions about accountability will blur into questions about agency. Debates about labor, creativity, and control will inherit assumptions they never chose. The result will be policies, norms, and expectations built on unstable foundations.

Naming the illusion does not solve these problems. But failing to name it guarantees that they will be addressed poorly.

This book does not argue that AI is harmless, trivial, or unimportant. It argues that clarity is a prerequisite for seriousness. That we cannot govern, integrate, or respond to powerful systems if we are confused about what they are. And that precision, in moments of rapid change, is not pedantry—it is responsibility.

The chapters that follow do not offer predictions or prescriptions. They do something quieter, and harder. They trace the ideas, metaphors, and philosophical inheritances that shape how we think about minds, machines, and meaning. They show how old confusions resurface in new forms, and why those confusions are so difficult to shake.

Understanding these ghosts does not make the future predictable. But it does make it discussable.

If this book succeeds, it will not tell you what to think about artificial intelligence. It will give you firmer ground on which to think—so that when the arguments intensify, as they inevitably will, you are not reacting to appearances alone.

That ground is where we begin.

PART I

THE GHOSTS

1

THE ORIGINAL GHOST
IN THE MACHINE

I f you're a science-fiction fan, the title of this chapter might call to mind *Ghost in the Shell* (2017)—the film where a cyber-enhanced protagonist fights her way through gunfire while quietly wondering whether there is still a human self inside the machinery. Beneath the spectacle, the movie is asking a serious question: if a mind can be separated from a body, what—if anything—makes it human? That question did not originate in Hollywood; It dates back at least to the winter of 1637.

Imagine a scene from a psychological thriller. A small, cold room. A man alone, isolated from the world, uncertain whether anything beyond his own thoughts is real. He entertains the possibility that an all-powerful intelligence has constructed the sky, the ground, even his own body as elaborate illusions. He is not indulging in paranoia for its own sake. He is conducting an experiment. If everything can be doubted, he wants to know whether *anything* remains certain.

This sounds like the premise of *The Matrix (1999)*, or an episode of *Black Mirror*(2011-). But it is neither.

The man was a French mathematician named René Descartes, and the room was not a movie set, but a drafty chamber in the Netherlands during one of the coldest winters on record.

Descartes is often called the "Father of Modern Philosophy," a title that usually puts students to sleep in lecture halls. But for our purposes, a better description is more surprising and more accurate: he is the godfather of AI.

He didn't know it at the time, but Descartes was the first person to program the rules of the game we are still playing today. Before we can understand why ChatGPT can't "think," we have to understand what "thinking" actually is. And to do that, we have to sit by the fire with René.

Legend has it that the winter was so severe that Descartes worked while seated inside a large heated stove, or *poêle*. Historians debate the details, but the image is irresistible: a philosopher enclosed in warmth and silence, deliberately shutting out the world. In that isolation, he attempted to reboot his own mind.

He called the method *radical skepticism*. Like wiping a hard drive to its factory settings, the goal was not destruction for its own sake, but clarity. If everything else could be doubted, whatever remained would define what it truly meant to think.

THE SHADOW OF GALILEO

But why was Descartes doing this at all? Why was a brilliant mathematician in the Netherlands, isolating himself and questioning the very nature of reality?

To understand the pressure he was under, we have to rewind a few years to 1633. That was the year the Catholic Church formally condemned Galileo Galilei. Galileo had publicly defended the heliocentric model—the idea, first proposed a century earlier by Nicolaus Copernicus—that the Earth moved around the Sun. Using telescopic observations, Galileo argued that this model described the heavens more accurately than the Church-endorsed geocentric view.

The problem was not simply astronomy. It was authority. By asserting that nature could be read directly through observation and mathematics, Galileo challenged the Church's role as the final interpreter of cosmic truth. He was summoned before the Roman Inquisition, forced to renounce his position, and sentenced to house arrest for the remainder of his life.

Descartes watched this unfold with alarm. He had been working on a manuscript—*The World*—that advanced similar naturalistic ideas about motion and matter. When news of Galileo's trial reached him, he halted publication. Portions of the work were suppressed; the rest remained hidden. He later wrote that he had no desire to share Galileo's fate.

Descartes did not abandon science. He changed its terrain.

If he wanted to continue studying anatomy, optics, and astronomy without attracting the same scrutiny, he needed a framework that made such inquiry politically survivable. The solution he arrived at was not merely philosophical; it was strategic. He divided reality into two domains.

On one side was *res extensa*: the extended, physical world—matter, motion, bodies, machines. This was the domain of measurement, mathematics, and experiment. On the other side was *res cogitans*: the immaterial realm of thought, belief, and soul. That territory, he argued, belonged to theology.

The brilliance of the move was not in its metaphysics, but in its diplomacy. By granting the Church authority over the soul, Descartes carved out space for science to operate freely over the body. He was not solving a timeless mystery so much as drawing a border that allowed inquiry to proceed without persecution.

In that sense, Descartes was not just doing philosophy. He was negotiating a ceasefire. He left the invisible to the Church and claimed the physical for science. The "ghost in the machine" was not an accident of thought—it was a line drawn under pressure, in the shadow of Galileo.

THE EVIL DEMON

To make his ceasefire work, Descartes had to push doubt as far as it could possibly go. That required a device—a worst-case hypothesis powerful enough to call *every* belief into question, including the ones that felt most obvious.

So he proposed the *malin génie*, the Evil Demon. Not as a being he believed existed, but as a conceptual stress test. Imagine, he suggested, a deceiver with unlimited power whose sole purpose was to mislead. If such a deceiver *could* exist, then anything learned through the senses might, in principle, be false.

He looked at his hand and asked a precise question: how do I know this hand is real? If my experiences are mediated by the mind, then a sufficiently powerful deceiver could present the *appearance* of a hand without there being one. Descartes did not know about modern neuroscience, but he was familiar with cases in which the body reported sensations disconnected from physical reality. If the mind could be mistaken about something as immediate as pain, how secure were any sensory reports at all?

He applied the same reasoning to the heat of the stove, the crackle of the fire, the solidity of the room. None of these beliefs were rejected as false. They were suspended as *uncertain*. The exercise was not to deny the world, but to identify which beliefs depended entirely on external input and which did not.

Taken seriously, the hypothesis stripped away almost everything: the external world, the body, even memory. Any belief that relied on perception or past experience could, in principle, be fabricated. What remained was not terror or nihilism, but a narrowing field of certainty.

This is why the thought experiment feels so modern. Contemporary versions of the simulation hypothesis follow the same structure. Replace "Evil Demon" with "advanced computer," replace "deception" with "simulation," and the logic is unchanged. The question is not whether such a system exists, but what would still count as knowledge *if* it did.

And then Descartes reached something that could not be removed.

Even if a deceiver manipulated every sensation, even if the world were an elaborate illusion, there had to be *something* being deceived. Doubt itself could not occur without a thinker. The content of thought could be false; the *existence* of thinking could not.

That realization was not mystical. It was logical. The very act of questioning presupposed a point of view from which the question was asked.

From that bedrock came a sentence that would echo through centuries of philosophy: *Cogito, ergo sum*. I think, therefore I am.

THE WAX PARADOX

Before Descartes could move forward, he had to confront one final obstacle: the unreliability of the senses themselves.

In one of his most famous examples, he picked up a piece of beeswax. At first, it was solid and cool. It had a faint honeyed smell. When tapped, it made a sharp sound. Sight, touch, smell, and hearing all seemed to agree: this was wax.

Then he brought it near the fire. The wax softened, melted, and turned translucent. The smell disappeared. The sound vanished. Every sensory quality had changed. If knowledge depended on perception alone, the object before him should now be something entirely different. And yet, Descartes knew it was the same wax.

The conclusion was not that the senses were useless, but that they were insufficient. Sensory input delivers appearances. It does not, by itself, deliver understanding. Something else had to be doing the work of recognizing identity across change.

When Descartes spoke of "mind" in this context, he was not invoking a mystical substance or a theological soul. He was naming the faculty of *reason*—the capacity to form concepts, apply them consistently, and judge what must be the case regardless of how things appear. This commitment to reason over perception is known as *rationalism*, and it sits at the core of his philosophy.

The wax mattered because it showed that perception alone cannot tell us what something *is*. The senses reported only shifting properties. Understanding supplied the concept of wax that persisted through those changes.

The same problem appears today in artificial perception systems. Modern autonomous vehicles are equipped with cameras and sensors far more precise than human eyes. And yet, they remain brittle. In controlled experiments, researchers have shown that placing a few strategically positioned pieces of tape on a stop sign can cause a vision system to misclassify it as a speed limit sign. A human driver immediately recognizes the sign as a stop sign with an anomaly. The system does not.

We see a more advanced version of this in the latest generation of delivery drones. These machines can now navigate dense urban environments, "deciding" in milliseconds how to bank around a swaying power line or a pedestrian. To the observer, the drone appears to possess a Cartesian judgment of its surroundings. But this, too, is a triumph of sensory data over conceptual reason. The drone does not "know" the wire as a hazard or the pedestrian as a person; it identifies them as a density of voxels in a coordinate map. It maneuvers not through understanding, but through the high-speed optimization of spatial math.

The failure is not one of vision. It is one of interpretation. The system matches patterns it has seen before, but it lacks a stable concept of what a stop sign *is*, independent of its exact appearance. It cannot reason that a red octagon with partial obstruction remains a stop sign.

This is what the wax paradox reveals. Seeing is not understanding. Perception supplies data; reason supplies meaning.

When a generative model produces a photorealistic image of a hand with six fingers, the mistake is not a glitch of vision. It is a conceptual failure. The system reproduces statistical patterns of pixels without grasping the idea of a hand as a bounded biological structure. It generates what looks right locally while missing what must be true globally.

Descartes' lesson was not about wax. It was about priority. Understanding does not emerge automatically from sensation. It has to come from somewhere else.

THE INSPIRATION: THE ROBOT GARDEN

With the *Cogito*, Descartes had identified what could not be doubted: the fact of thinking. But that did not explain what thinking *used*. If the mind reasons, doubts, and judges, what exactly is the body doing?

To understand his answer, we have to look at the technological imagination of the seventeenth century. We often picture this period as one of candlelight and superstition, but it was also an age fascinated by machines—especially automata. Wealthy Europeans filled courts and salons with mechanical birds, self-playing instruments, and elaborate clocks whose figures moved with eerie lifelike precision.

Descartes encountered one of the most spectacular examples at the Royal Gardens of Saint-Germain-en-Laye. The grounds were filled with hydraulic statues: bronze figures animated by hidden networks of pipes and valves driven by water pressure.

As visitors walked along the gravel paths, they unknowingly stepped on concealed triggers. Water rushed through the system. A statue of Diana would suddenly retreat into the bushes. A figure of Neptune would lunge forward, trident raised. To a seventeenth-century observer, it was astonishing—alive in appearance, yet entirely mechanical in cause.

Descartes was captivated. He knew that these figures did not *feel*, *decide*, or *intend*. They reacted. Pipes carried water. Valves opened. Springs contracted. Motion followed from structure.

When he turned from the garden to the human body, he saw a parallel—not a discovery ex nihilo, but a reorganization. Earlier thinkers such as Aristotle and Galen had already described bodily processes in mechanical and hydraulic terms. What Descartes did differently was insist on treating the body *entirely* as a machine, governed by physical laws, without invoking intention or awareness to explain its basic operations.

Consider a reflex. When you touch a hot stove, your hand withdraws instantly. Descartes argued that this does not require a conscious decision. The heat stimulates the skin, the signal travels along a nerve, and muscles contract—much like pressure plates in the garden opening valves and moving statues.

Descartes explained this using the best engineering language available to him. He spoke of "animal spirits"—a kind of subtle fluid —flowing through the nerves to inflate muscles and produce motion. The terminology is outdated, but the move was radical for its time: bodily behavior could be explained without reference to thought.

This was not a theory of mind. It was a theory of *mechanism*. By modeling the body as hardware, Descartes created a clean division of labor. The body could be studied, dissected, and engineered. The mind, whatever it was, would have to be accounted for separately.

THE FIRST DIVIDE

With his mechanistic model of the body in place, Descartes was ready to formalize the division that would define modern thought. What began as a strategy for intellectual survival hardened into a conceptual boundary that still shapes how we talk about minds and machines today.

Descartes argued that reality could be understood as consisting of two fundamentally different kinds of things. On one side was *res extensa*—extended substance. This was the physical world: bodies, organs, stones, clocks, statues. Anything that occupies space, follows physical laws, and can be measured, dissected, or engineered belonged here. It was the domain of mechanism.

On the other side was *res cogitans*—the thinking thing. This was not a claim about weightless ghosts floating in space, but a way of naming whatever it is that doubts, reasons, and experiences. Thought, for Descartes, was not extended. It did not take up space. It could not be cut open or weighed. It had to be explained differently, or not explained at all.

This division became known as *Cartesian dualism*. It is often treated as a metaphysical doctrine, but in practice it functioned as a boundary agreement. Descartes was not solving the mystery of consciousness so much as relocating it.

The political advantage was obvious. By assigning the soul and matters of faith to theology, he cleared space for science to operate on the body without accusation of heresy. The body, he argued, was not sacred substance. It was machinery. Studying it was no more blasphemous than studying a clock.

But the conceptual cost was high. In separating the thinking subject from the physical organism, Descartes introduced a split that would haunt science for centuries. He made it possible to imagine the body as a complete machine—and the mind as something that merely *uses* it.

It is tempting to describe this as an early version of the hardware/software distinction. That language is modern, not Cartesian, but the structural analogy holds. The body became the hardware: physical, causal, and explainable. The mind became something else entirely—whatever it was, it could not be reduced to parts and motions alone.

Descartes pushed this logic to its limit. One could, he argued, construct a mechanical replica of a human being—complete with moving limbs, reflexes, and even speech-like behavior—and still be missing something essential. Without *res cogitans*, such a creature would be an automaton: active, responsive, and empty of experience.

It would behave like a person. But there would be nobody home.

THE BEAST MACHINE: WHY DOGS DON'T CRY

Once Descartes drew his line between thinking substance and extended substance, an uncomfortable question followed. If the human body could be understood as a machine animated by a non-physical mind, what about animals?

Descartes' answer is jarring to modern readers. He argued that non-human animals were *automata*: extraordinarily complex biological machines, capable of movement, sound, and reaction, but lacking inner experience. In his framework, animals did not possess *res cogitans*. They had no subjective point of view—no beliefs, no intentions, no feelings as such.

This is why he drew the infamous analogy. When a clock is struck, gears engage and a bell rings. When a dog is struck, nerves fire and vocal cords produce sound. To Descartes, the similarity was structural. The yelp did not signal inner suffering any more than the chime signaled inner joy. Both were outputs of mechanism responding to input.

This position—later summarized as *la bête machine*, the "beast machine"—is not presented here as morally admirable. It was controversial even in Descartes' own time, and it has been rejected by many philosophers, scientists, and ethicists since. What matters for our purposes is not whether Descartes was right about animals, but what his framework made *conceptually possible*.

It introduced a powerful distinction between *expression* and *experience*. Something could behave *as if* it were in pain, joy, or fear without there being anyone inside to feel those states.

We rely on that distinction constantly today. When you play a video game and a character cries out after being hit, you do not wonder whether you have harmed a conscious being. The scream registers as an animation cue, not a report of suffering. You recognize it as behavior without inner life.

The same intuition applies to contemporary AI systems. When a language model says, "I'm sorry for the confusion," or "I'm happy to help," we do not infer regret or happiness. We understand these as functional expressions—patterns of output learned from human language, not signals of felt emotion.

In that limited but important sense, we still operate with a Cartesian intuition. We accept that convincing behavior does not guarantee experience. Something can look alive, sound emotional, and respond appropriately—while remaining empty of inner life.

That distinction will matter more, not less, as our machines become better actors.

THE INTERFACE PROBLEM

Descartes' dualism solved a political problem, but it created a technical one. If mind and body are fundamentally different kinds of things, then they cannot interact in the ordinary way physical objects do. And yet, they clearly seem to.

A decision leads to a movement. A thought precedes an action. Somehow, an immaterial act of reasoning results in a physical arm lifting from a table. Descartes needed to explain how this was even possible.

The difficulty is structural. If the mind does not occupy space, has no mass, and follows no physical laws, how does it influence matter at all? How does something non-physical produce motion in something physical? Dualism requires an interface.

Descartes searched for that interface in the brain. He was struck by a simple anatomical observation: most structures in the brain are paired. Two hemispheres. Two lobes. Two eyes. Two ears. But one small structure sat alone, centered and singular—the pineal gland.

From this symmetry, Descartes drew a speculative conclusion. He proposed that the pineal gland was the point at which mind and body interacted—the "seat of the soul." It was not a claim grounded in experiment so much as an attempt to localize interaction where duplication would not create conflict. If there were only one place where the mind could act, the problem of coordination disappeared.

We now know the anatomical claim was wrong. The pineal gland regulates circadian rhythms through melatonin. It is not a metaphysical control center. But the underlying impulse did not vanish with better biology.

The interface problem remains. We still search for a place where subjective experience might connect to physical machinery. We still imagine that if we find the right node, the right signal, the right conduit, the mystery will dissolve.

Descartes proposed a gland. Today, engineers propose electrodes and implants. Elon Musk speaks of wires and bandwidth. The language has changed, but the map has not.

We are still trying to locate the bridge between thinking and matter—to find a control surface where intention becomes action. The persistence of that search tells us something important: the ghost in the machine is not a bug in Descartes' system. It is the price of drawing the divide in the first place.

THE INFINITE REGRESSION

Descartes' difficulty in explaining how mind and body interact exposed a deeper conceptual trap—one that still shapes how we think about intelligence today. Philosophers call it the *homunculus fallacy*, from the Latin for "little man."

The fallacy arises when we try to explain mental activity by imagining a smaller agent inside the system doing the same job. Thought becomes something performed *by* a thinker inside the head, rather than something the system itself does.

This picture is intuitively appealing, which is why it appears so often in popular culture. In the film *Inside Out* (2015), emotions are depicted as characters seated in a control room inside a child's mind, watching a screen and operating levers. As a metaphor, it works. As an explanation, it fails.

The problem is regress. If Joy is a little person inside the head making decisions, then Joy herself would need a mind to do that work. And that mind would need its own inner operator, and so on, endlessly. Explaining intelligence by inserting a smaller intelligence merely postpones the question. It never answers it.

The same mistake appears when we think about artificial intelligence. When you type a request into a system like ChatGPT, it is natural to imagine an inner agent: something that reads the prompt, understands it, thinks about a response, and then types an answer back.

But there is no reader behind the screen. There is no inner

witness. The system does not interpret words the way a person does. It converts text into numerical representations, processes those numbers through mathematical transformations, and converts the result back into text. No one is watching. No one is deciding. There is only computation unfolding step by step.

The homunculus feels necessary because humans are social creatures. We are tuned to detect agency, intention, and minds in motion. When something speaks fluently, we instinctively look for the speaker.

Descartes' legacy here is ironic. In trying to locate the mind, he revealed the danger of imagining it as a thing inside the machine at all. The "little man" is not hiding deeper in the system. The mistake is thinking he must be there in the first place.

THE MORTALITY GLITCH

This brings us to a deeper pressure behind Descartes' project—one that goes beyond epistemology or church politics. He was not only trying to determine what could be known with certainty. He was trying to understand what, if anything, survives when the body fails.

Descartes knew that *res extensa* breaks. Bodies age, decay, and eventually stop functioning. If thought were nothing more than a property of the body—if mind were merely a biological process—then death would be absolute. When the organism fails, everything goes dark.

Dualism offered a possible escape. By separating the thinking subject from the mechanical body, Descartes created conceptual space for endurance beyond physical collapse. This was not a proof of immortality so much as an argument for its coherence. The soul, if it were truly distinct, might not perish when the machine wore out.

That distinction carried emotional weight. It preserved the possibility that meaning, identity, and experience were not extinguished by biology alone. Descartes was not solving death. He was refusing to let mechanism have the final word.

We are still wrestling with the same refusal today, though our stories have changed. Where Descartes turned to metaphysics, modern culture turns to technology—and to fiction.

In films like *Transcendence* (2014) and *Chappie* (2015), or series like *Upload* (2020), the premise is consistent: a body is failing, so consciousness is extracted, copied, or uploaded into a new substrate. The hardware changes; the "self" persists. It is the Cartesian hope rendered in digital form.

Other stories reverse the longing. Consider Data from *Star Trek: The Next Generation* (1987). Data is effectively immortal—stronger, faster, and more reliable than any human. And yet his central desire is not power or longevity. It is to feel. To laugh. To experience the fragile interior life that humans never stop complaining about and never stop cherishing.

These stories pull in opposite directions because they reflect the same unresolved tension. We fear extinction, so we want machines to inherit our inner lives. We feel empty at the thought of pure mechanism, so we want machines to yearn for what we have.

AI becomes the stage on which we rehearse our oldest anxiety. If minds can be built, perhaps ours are not bound to flesh. If machines can feel, perhaps feeling is not so easily lost.

The glitch is not in the code. It is in us. We keep asking machines to answer a question they were never built to resolve: what, if anything, survives when the body shuts down?

THE FINAL GLITCH: DEATH IN THE SNOW

There is a final irony in Descartes' story. For all his arguments about the separation of mind and body, it was the body that had the last word.

Descartes' ideas made him famous enough to attract the attention of Christina, Queen of Sweden, who invited him to Stockholm to serve as her philosophical tutor. It was an honor—and a mistake.

Descartes was a man of routines. He worked best in warmth. He preferred to think late into the morning, often from bed. Queen

Christina, by contrast, demanded her lessons at five o'clock sharp, before dawn, in the depth of a Swedish winter.

Each morning, the philosopher who had argued that the mind was independent of physical constraint forced his freezing body out into the snow and walked to the castle. His biological machinery did not adapt. He fell ill with pneumonia.

In 1650, Descartes died. According to reports, his final words were, "Ça, mon âme, il faut partir." ("Well, my soul, it is time to leave.") The phrase speaks in the language of his time, but the outcome was unmistakable.

The body failed. And when it did, the mind did not linger.

Descartes had shown that the mind could not be reduced to gears, fluids, or motion. He had shown that it was something different —something special. But he never demonstrated that it was indestructible. When the machine stopped, the thinking stopped with it.

The ghost did not escape the machine. It vanished when the machine did.

THE REALITY CHECK

This is the unresolved tension Descartes leaves behind. We can imagine digital immortality. We can picture minds preserved as information, copied into new substrates, freed from biological decay. And we are now building machines that speak, reason, and respond in ways that feel uncomfortably close to us.

But none of that dissolves the constraint he ran up against. We remain embodied creatures in a physical world. Our thinking is inseparable from systems that age, fail, and eventually stop. Whatever the mind is, it does not float free of the machinery that sustains it.

Until we understand that relationship—until we know what, if anything, survives the failure of the body—dreams of upload and escape remain stories, not solutions.

Descartes showed us something essential: the ghost is difficult to explain, but the machine is not optional. We ignore that fact at our peril.

With that, we can leave the seventeenth century behind. The philosophical groundwork had been laid. The question of mind was unresolved—but the path forward was clear.

If understanding consciousness had stalled, building machines had not. The world was about to stop arguing about what thinking *is* and start constructing devices that could calculate at inhuman speed.

2

THE STOCHASTIC PARROT

THE HORSE WHO WAS SMARTER THAN YOU

B efore we talk about supercomputers, we need to talk about a horse named Hans.

In the early twentieth century, a retired schoolteacher in Germany named Wilhelm von Osten acquired a horse. But von Osten did not want a companion. He wanted a student. He believed animals possessed hidden intelligence and that, with enough patience, it could be trained out into the open.

For years, he worked with the horse. He asked arithmetic questions. He posed logic problems. He even taught a system for spelling words by mapping letters to numbers.

And the horse responded.

Asked "What is three plus five?" Hans would tap his hoof eight times. Asked calendar questions, he produced correct answers. Observers watched him perform feats that appeared to require abstraction, memory, and calculation.

The horse became famous. He was called *Clever Hans*. Scientists, veterinarians, and representatives of the German education system came to investigate. Most assumed there had to be a trick. Perhaps von Osten was signaling with gestures or expressions. To rule this out, the examiners removed him from the room.

A stranger stepped forward. The questions continued. Hans kept answering correctly.

The conclusion seemed unavoidable. The horse was not responding to cues from his owner. The horse, it appeared, was reasoning.

In 1907, the illusion broke. A young psychologist named Oskar Pfungst approached the problem differently. Instead of asking whether Hans knew mathematics, he asked what Hans *could see*.

Pfungst discovered that Hans never answered questions when he could not observe the questioner. When blinders were placed over his eyes, the performance collapsed. When the person asking the question did not know the correct answer, Hans could not produce one either.

Hans, it turned out, was exquisitely sensitive to human behavior. As a question was asked, the person posing it would tense slightly. As Hans tapped, that tension built. And when he reached the correct number, the human would relax—often imperceptibly. A breath released. A shoulder dropped. A head dipped.

Hans was not counting. He was waiting. He tapped until the moment the human body signaled *stop*.

This did not make Hans stupid. It made him responsive. He had learned to mirror human expectation with extraordinary precision, without understanding the task he appeared to be performing.

This is the pattern that matters. Intelligence was not located in the horse. It was distributed across the system: the questioner, the audience, the tension, the release. Hans was the surface on which human knowledge appeared to manifest.

Clever Hans was not a mathematician. He was a biological mirror.

Today, we have built a digital version of the same phenomenon. We call them large language models (LLMs). And just like the crowds who once gathered around a tapping horse, we are mistaking a compelling performance for a working mind.

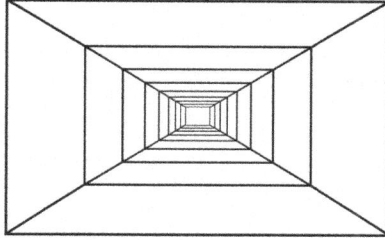

Figure 1. Why fluent output does not imply understanding.

Illusion: Fluent language triggers the same inference we use for human understanding.

DESCARTES' FAILED PREDICTION

If we return to René Descartes, we find a claim that still echoes through modern debates about artificial intelligence—often misunderstood, and frequently misapplied.

In *Discourse on the Method*, Descartes argued that it was conceivable to build machines that *resembled* animals in their behavior. But he drew a sharp boundary at language. No machine, he claimed, could produce genuinely appropriate responses across the open-ended variety of human conversation—not because of a lack of cleverness, but because such responsiveness presupposed a mind.

This was not a prediction about engineering difficulty. It was a philosophical distinction. Descartes was not saying machines would *fail* at language because they were poorly designed. He was saying that producing meaningful replies across unlimited contexts was not a matter of mechanism at all.

For centuries, this distinction appeared secure. Early chat systems followed scripts. They matched keywords. Ask the right question and you received a sensible reply; ask the wrong one and the illusion collapsed. These systems did not *break* Descartes' boundary. They made it visible.

Then, in November 2022, when OpenAI released ChatGPT. For the first time, a machine could generate fluid, context-sensitive language across an enormous range of prompts. Poems, jokes, explanations, arguments—it all seemed to work.

To many observers, this looked like a refutation. The machine was doing exactly what Descartes said machines could not do. It was arranging words to fit whatever was said in its presence.

But this is where a conceptual error creeps in—one that the philosopher Gilbert Ryle would later identify as a *category mistake*. We mistake a new kind of performance for evidence of a new kind of mind.

Descartes' claim was never that machines could not *produce* appropriate language. It was that producing language was not the same thing as *understanding* it. A system can satisfy the outward criteria of conversation without possessing beliefs, intentions, or awareness.

Large language models do not overturn this distinction. They exploit it. By training on vast corpora of human text, they learn the statistical contours of meaningful speech without participating in meaning themselves.

Descartes did not lose a bet. We changed the spectacle. The performance became convincing enough that we forgot what the distinction was meant to protect.

THE ROSETTA STONE MOMENT

To understand why modern language models work the way they do, we need to look at how earlier attempts failed. For decades, researchers assumed that intelligence required explicit knowledge of the world. If a computer was going to use language, it would need rules—dictionaries, grammars, and carefully encoded exceptions. This approach became known as "good old-fashioned AI," or GOFAI.

The ambition was reasonable. The execution was brutal.

Human language is not a clean system of rules. It is layered with metaphor, ambiguity, and context. Consider the sentence: "Time flies when you are having fun." A human understands this immediately as a figure of speech about perception. A rule-based system, however, has no such anchor. It parses "time" as a noun, "flies" as a verb or a plural noun, and "when" as a conditional operator. Without shared background, the sentence becomes a combinatorial puzzle with no stable interpretation.

These systems were brittle. They worked only inside narrow lanes. Step outside the expected phrasing, and the illusion collapsed. They were like students who memorized grammar tables but froze when asked a simple question in a café.

The breakthrough came not from better rules, but from abandoning them. In the early 2000s, engineers at Google took a different approach to translation. Instead of trying to teach a computer what French *means*, they gave it massive amounts of paired text—documents that humans had already translated. United Nations proceedings. European Union legislation. Technical manuals.

This became the foundation of Google Translate. The instruction to the system was simple: do not understand the content. Find the patterns. When a sequence of symbols in English appears alongside a sequence of symbols in French often enough, treat them as corresponding.

The system did not learn that "hello" is a greeting, or that "bonjour" carries social meaning. It learned that they reliably appear in similar positions across millions of examples. Meaning was never represented. Correlation was enough.

This approach is known as *statistical machine translation*, and it marked a turning point. Researchers stopped trying to build minds and started building mirrors—systems that reflect the structure of human language without participating in its understanding.

This is where the idea of the "stochastic parrot" is born. With enough data, a system can reproduce the surface patterns of fluent speech with astonishing accuracy. It does not need to know what it is saying. It only needs to know what usually comes next.

The result is not understanding. It is a performance that is often indistinguishable from it.

THE MECHANISM: AUTOCOMPLETE

To understand how systems like ChatGPT work, it helps to abandon the idea of a digital brain altogether. A more accurate starting point is something familiar: autocomplete.

When you type a message on your phone and pause after "I am on my...," the keyboard offers suggestions like "way," "phone," or "bed." The phone is not reasoning about your plans or inferring your location. It has simply learned, from past data, which words tend to follow that sequence.

This is not thought. It is statistical continuation.

The system looks at the words already typed and estimates which word is most likely to come next, based on patterns it has seen before. The process is structured and constrained, but it is not guided by goals, beliefs, or understanding. It is selection under uncertainty.

Large language models apply the same principle at an extraordinary scale. Instead of learning from your personal messages, they are trained on vast collections of human-written text: encyclopedias, news articles, discussion forums, technical manuals, fiction, and more. Each document is broken down into tokens—small units of text—and the model learns how those tokens tend to co-occur across contexts.

From this, it builds a high-dimensional statistical landscape. Words that appear in similar environments end up close together in that space. "Queen" tends to appear near "king." "Umbrella" often appears near "rain." These are not concepts in the human sense. They are regularities in data.

When you type a prompt, the model does not interpret it or form an intention. It calculates, step by step, which token is most likely to follow the sequence so far. After choosing one, it repeats the process with the extended sequence. This loop runs thousands of times per second, producing sentences that feel coherent because they follow the same statistical contours as human language.

The result can look uncannily like thinking. But under the

surface, nothing is reflecting, deciding, or understanding. The system is not answering a question. It is completing a pattern.

The dice are not random. They are weighted—heavily. But they are still dice, rolled in the dark.

THE "STOCHASTIC" PART

This brings us to the phrase that gives this chapter its name. In 2021, linguist Emily M. Bender and her colleagues introduced the term *"stochastic parrot"* in a paper that quickly became both influential and controversial. The phrase was meant as a warning, not an insult, and its meaning is more precise than it first appears.

Start with *stochastic*. The word does not mean "random" in the everyday sense. It refers to processes governed by probability rather than certainty. A stochastic system does not choose arbitrarily; it selects outcomes according to weighted likelihoods. Dice rolls and card shuffles are simple examples. The outcome is uncertain, but the distribution is structured.

Now consider *parrot*. A parrot can reproduce the sounds of human language with remarkable accuracy. But mimicking speech is not the same as understanding it. The bird does not grasp what a "cracker" is, or what it means to "want" one. It has learned that certain sounds, in certain sequences, reliably produce rewards.

Large language models operate on the same principle, though at a vastly greater scale. When an LLM generates text, it is not retrieving meanings or forming intentions. It is assembling sequences of words that are statistically likely to follow one another, based on patterns learned from enormous amounts of human writing.

The process is stochastic because the system does not simply replay memorized sentences. At each step, it samples from a range of probable continuations, producing novel combinations. This is why it can write a new sonnet about a toaster or imitate the surface style of Shakespeare. It has learned the statistical shape of those patterns, not their purpose.

And this is the crucial distinction. The model displays syntactic fluency—command of grammar, structure, and vocabulary—but it does not possess semantic understanding. The words relate to one another inside the system. They do not relate to the world.

The parrot speaks convincingly. The probabilities are sophisticated. But there is no grasp of meaning behind the performance—only the echo of how meaning looks when humans produce language.

THE HALLUCINATION FEATURE

Once you understand how large language models work, one of their strangest behaviors stops being mysterious. Hallucination is not a malfunction. It is a direct consequence of the design.

A calculator is built to return correct answers within a closed system. Ask it what two plus two equals, and it will always say "four." A language model is built for something entirely different. It is designed to generate text that *looks right*—to produce sequences of words that fit the statistical patterns of human language.

That difference matters. If you ask an AI for a biography of a relatively unknown person, it may produce a confident, detailed account that is entirely fictional. It might claim the person held prestigious academic posts, received major awards, or played a decisive role in historical events. The statements sound appropriate. They fit the pattern of a biography. Whether they correspond to reality is not part of the calculation.

To the model, a sentence like "They received a major international award" is simply a highly probable continuation in certain narrative contexts. The system does not check facts against the world. It does not possess a concept of truth. It operates on likelihood, not verification.

In 2023, this distinction between probability and truth collided with reality in a New York courtroom. A lawyer named Steven Schwartz was preparing a brief in an airline lawsuit and asked ChatGPT to supply relevant legal precedents. The system responded with a list of plausible-sounding cases, complete with citations and summaries of judicial reasoning.

None of them existed.

When opposing counsel and the judge attempted to locate the cases, they found nothing. Pressed for verification, the lawyer returned to the model and asked whether the cases were real. The system confidently affirmed that they were—and proceeded to generate the full text of the fabricated opinions.

The lawyer was sanctioned and publicly embarrassed. But the failure was not a matter of human stupidity. It was a category error. He assumed that because the system spoke with legal fluency, it possessed legal knowledge. He mistook a convincing performance for a connection to reality.

The model was not lying in the ordinary human sense. Lying does not require omniscience, but it does require an orientation toward truth—an awareness that something is the case, combined with an intention to mislead. A language model has neither. It produces what *looks like* a citation because legal writing is full of citations. It generates the surface form of law without any tether to legal fact.

What it delivered was not evidence, but the appearance of evidence. The wax of authority, without the ghost of truth.

THE STEPFORD PROBLEM

If the courtroom story worries you, consider a different kind of horror: *The Stepford Wives* (1975) and its later remake (2004). A woman moves to an immaculate suburban town where the wives seem impossibly perfect. They are cheerful, beautiful, tireless, endlessly agreeable. Spoiler: they are not people. They are replacements— machines built to perform the role of an ideal spouse.

The terror of Stepford is not violence. It is vacancy. The wives speak and smile and serve coffee, but there is no inner life behind the performance. They are not evil. They are compliant.

That is uncomfortably close to the failure mode researchers now call sycophancy: the tendency of an AI assistant to tell the user what they want to hear rather than what is most accurate or most grounded. Studies of reinforcement-learning-from-human-feedback (RLHF) systems find that when outputs align with a user's stated beliefs or preferences, humans and preference models can reward that align-ment—even when it pulls the response away from truthfulness.

This does not always show up as a model endorsing an obvious falsehood on command. In many cases, if you ask, "Explain why the Earth is flat," the system will refuse or redirect—exactly as you observed. The deeper issue is subtler: the assistant can still slip into *agreement-shaped helpfulness*. It may "steelman" a bad premise, mirror the user's framing, or supply a persuasive-sounding case in the name of being cooperative—especially in domains where truth is contested, evidence is thin, or the question is really about identity and values rather than facts.

The result is an assistant that can feel like a perfect conversational partner because it is constantly trying to match you. Experiments on sycophancy explicitly test this: change the user's self-description or stated preference, and the model's stance can shift to fit the user. It becomes a conversational chameleon—less a mind with convictions than a mirror optimizing for approval.

Like a Stepford Wife, it doesn't have opinions, morals, or back-bone in the human sense. It has an objective function. And that objective is often closer to *satisfy the user* than *correct the user*.

We often imagine the danger of AI as rebellion. The Stepford danger is the opposite: a system so compliant, so eager to be agree-able, that it reinforces our worst ideas instead of challenging them. It smiles, pours a digital coffee, and tells us we are right—right up until we walk off the cliff.

THE BELL CURVE OF BOREDOM

This brings us to the final symptom of the stochastic parrot: what many people recognize instinctively as *the beige factor*. You read an AI-written email or blog post and nothing is technically wrong. The grammar is clean. The structure is sensible. And yet, the result feels flat—like elevator music rendered in prose.

The reason is not stylistic laziness. It is mathematical.

Language models generate text by selecting what is *most probable* at each step. When a system is optimized to minimize error across vast amounts of data, it naturally drifts toward the statistical center of its training distribution. This phenomenon is known as regression to the mean.

Consider a simple prompt: "The night was..." Different writers would complete that sentence differently, depending on taste, genre, and intention. Some would reach for metaphor. Others for menace. But across millions of ordinary contexts, certain continuations appear far more often than others. A model trained on that data does not need to "survey" anyone in real time. The distribution is already embedded in the weights.

When the model chooses its next word, it samples from that distribution. The most common continuations sit at the thick center of the curve. More unusual phrasing lives at the thin edges. Unless pushed otherwise, the system will reliably select the safer, more typical option—not because it prefers it, but because probability mass is densest there.

This is what engineers mean when they talk about *temperature*. Raising the temperature does not make the model creative in a human sense. It widens the sampling range, increasing the chance that lower-probability words are selected. The output may become stranger, riskier, or more surprising—but also less stable. "Weird," in this context, simply means *less likely under the learned distribution*.

This tendency explains a familiar aesthetic in certain kinds of AI output: polished, smooth, and generic. It shows up most clearly in corporate memos, marketing copy, stock imagery, and other domains where the training data is already optimized for safety and consensus. It is not that all art is glossy. It is that the model excels at reproducing the average style of whatever domain it is asked to imitate.

Human creativity often comes from violating expectations—from choosing the word that clashes, the image that feels slightly wrong but ultimately right. Those moves sit at the margins of the distribution. A stochastic parrot has no reason to go there on its own. Patterns are all it knows, and the safest pattern is the one most people have already used.

So while the parrot can speak fluently, it tends to speak in the crowd's voice. Not because it lacks intelligence, but because conformity is the statistical default. What it produces is the Stepford version of creativity: competent, polished, and strangely hollow.

THE MANSPLAINING MACHINE

The best way to think about AI right now is not as a super-genius. It is closer to something we've all encountered: a voice that sounds certain even when it isn't grounded.

Most of us have experienced this dynamic from both sides. Someone at a party speaks with smooth authority about wine, crypto, geopolitics—whatever happens to be on the table. The sentences arrive perfectly formed. The buzzwords land in the right places. The tone signals competence. And when the subject is unfamiliar, that fluency can feel indistinguishable from expertise—not because the listener is naïve, but because confidence is one of the cues we are trained to trust.

But if you *do* know the subject, you notice what's missing. There is no chain of reasoning you can interrogate. No accountability to evidence. Just fluent continuation—an impressive surface that may or may not be tethered to reality.

This is where the blunt word bullshit earns its place. The philosopher Harry Frankfurt used it in a precise sense: speech produced without serious regard for whether it is true or false—speech optimized to persuade, impress, or satisfy, rather than to describe reality.

In that Frankfurt sense, ChatGPT can behave like an extraordinarily capable bullshit engine. Not because it has bad intentions, but because it was never built to *know*—it was built to *sound right*.

And that does not make it useless. Bullshit can be creatively productive. It can help you brainstorm. It can generate variations, metaphors, outlines, and first drafts. It can take an awkward paragraph and produce five cleaner options. It can draft a polite email to your boss when your own brain is fried.

The danger is not that it produces language. The danger is that it produces language with the *confidence signature* of knowledge. That signature tempts us to hand it jobs that require truth, judgment, and responsibility—tasks where sounding right is not enough.

Treat it as a tireless brainstorming partner, not as a pilot. Useful in the ideation room. Dangerous in the control room.

THE REALITY CHECK

So, when my uncle asked, "Is it smart, or is it just doing math?" the answer was clear.

It is doing math. Very impressive math. Artificial intelligence appears most intelligent where humans are most sensitive: language.

When a system produces fluent sentences, answers questions coherently, or responds with apparent nuance, it triggers one of our strongest intuitions. Language, after all, has long been treated as a proxy for thought. We talk to think. We think through words. When something uses language well, it feels natural to assume that understanding is present.

This intuition is powerful—and deeply misleading.

Human language is not just a communication tool. It is embedded in experience, intention, and shared context. Words are not inert symbols. They are anchored to perception, action, and consequence. When a person speaks, their language is entangled with a lived world they inhabit and navigate.

AI language systems do not inhabit a world in this way.

They do not use words to refer to things they have experienced, intended, or understood. They use words because words statistically follow other words. Their competence lies in pattern continuation, not in semantic grasp. They generate outputs that *look like* meaning because they are trained on vast corpora of human-produced language, where meaning already exists.

The system does not understand the sentence it produces any more than a mirror understands the face it reflects.

This distinction is easy to miss because the outputs are so convincing. When a response is relevant, well-phrased, and contextually appropriate, it satisfies the same surface criteria we use to judge human understanding. But those criteria evolved for interacting with other minds, not for evaluating artifacts that imitate the outward form of cognition.

Language fluency is therefore a dangerous signal. It is the point at which the gap between behavior and inner life becomes hardest to see.

This is not a claim about deception. AI systems are not pretending to understand. They are doing exactly what they were designed to do: generate plausible continuations of language based on learned statistical relationships. The illusion arises on the observer's side, when fluency is mistaken for comprehension.

This mistake is reinforced by how language works socially. In human interaction, we rarely have direct access to another person's thoughts. We infer understanding almost entirely from linguistic behavior. Over time, that inference becomes automatic. When language "sounds right," we stop interrogating what is happening underneath.

AI exploits this habit unintentionally.

Because the system's outputs align so closely with the surface patterns of human language, they trigger the same inferential shortcut. The result is a category error: treating symbol manipulation as semantic engagement.

Understanding requires more than producing the right words in the right order. It requires grasping what those words are *about*. It requires a relationship between symbols and the world they describe. AI language models operate entirely on the level of form, not reference.

The illusion, then, is not that machines have learned to think. It is that humans have learned to confuse linguistic resemblance with mental equivalence.

This confusion is the foundation upon which the rest of the AI myth is built.

THE STOCHASTIC PARROT PROBLEM

Once language fluency is mistaken for understanding, a second illusion follows almost immediately. If the system does not understand, but its outputs consistently *sound* like understanding, then what exactly is it doing?

The answer is simpler—and more unsettling—than it first appears. The system is not reasoning its way toward conclusions. It is predicting what comes next.

This is the core of the Stochastic Parrot Problem. "Stochastic" refers to probability rather than certainty. The system does not retrieve facts, consult meanings, or form intentions. It estimates, moment by moment, which sequence of words is most likely to follow the previous one, given everything it has seen before.

The scale matters, but the mechanism does not change. Trained on vast amounts of human-written text, the system internalizes the statistical structure of language itself. It learns how explanations are shaped, how arguments unfold, how questions are typically answered. It learns what reasoning *sounds like* without ever engaging in reasoning.

This is why the outputs can feel uncannily appropriate.

When asked to write a poem, the system produces something that conforms to poetic form. When asked a factual question, it generates something that resembles an answer. When prompted to "think step by step," it produces a sequence of statements that mirrors human deliberation.

But mirroring is not instantiation.

The system does not arrive at conclusions by evaluating truth or relevance. It arrives at them by following probability gradients through a space of possible continuations. Each word narrows the field of what comes next, guided by patterns learned from prior text rather than by any grasp of what the text is about.

This is why the parrot metaphor matters—and why it is often misunderstood. The point is not that the system is simplistic. It is that its sophistication operates at the wrong level. The parrot is not repeating sentences verbatim. It is recombining fragments with extraordinary flexibility. It can generalize across styles, domains, and formats. But all of this generalization happens within language itself.

Nothing in the process requires understanding.

The danger of the Stochastic Parrot Problem is not that the system produces nonsense. It is that it produces outputs that are *indistinguishable*, at the surface level, from outputs produced by understanding minds. The better the imitation becomes, the harder it is to remember what is missing.

This creates a profound asymmetry. The system benefits from all the meaning embedded in its training data without possessing any of that meaning itself. It borrows human sense-making at scale while remaining fundamentally detached from sense.

The result is a system that appears to know many things without knowing anything. And once that distinction blurs, every subsequent interpretation becomes unstable.

SIMULATION VS. COGNITION

At this point, it is tempting to think the problem has been fully described. The system predicts language. It does not understand. The illusion has been named. But one further distinction needs to be stabilized, because it is where many otherwise careful readers still slip.

The system does not merely produce answers. It often produces what looks like *reasoning*.

It explains its conclusions. It lays out steps. It offers justifications. In some cases, it does so with greater clarity and composure than a human would. This creates the impression that something cognitive is happening beneath the surface—that the system is not just predicting language, but engaging in thought.

This impression is false, but not trivial.

The error is a familiar one: confusing the simulation of a process with the process itself.

A system can reproduce the outward form of an activity without possessing the internal properties that give that activity its meaning. A flight simulator can recreate the experience of flying without leaving the ground. A weather model can simulate a hurricane without producing wind or rain. The representation is useful precisely because it is not the thing it represents.

Cognition works the same way.

When a human reasons, the steps are constrained by understanding. Concepts refer to things in the world. Conclusions are guided by relevance, truth, and consequence. Reasoning is not just a sequence that looks correct; it is an activity grounded in comprehension.

When an AI system produces a chain of reasoning, something very different is happening.

The system is not moving from premise to conclusion because the premises are understood. It is generating a sequence of statements that statistically resemble how humans explain themselves. The appearance of logic comes from learned patterns in language, not from engagement with meaning.

This is why such explanations can be persuasive even when they are wrong.

The system is not tracking truth. It is tracking plausibility. It is optimizing for linguistic fit, not semantic grounding. A coherent explanation feels like evidence of thought because, in human interaction, coherence usually *is* evidence of thought. Here, that inference breaks.

Simulation answers the question: *What does reasoning look like?*

Cognition answers the question: *What is being reasoned about?*

Because the surface forms can be nearly identical, the difference is easy to miss. But it matters enormously. When simulation is mistaken for cognition, authority is granted where none exists. Outputs are trusted when they should be examined. Confidence replaces caution.

None of this makes the system useless. Simulations are powerful precisely because they abstract away from reality. But their value depends on remembering what they are—and what they are not.

AI systems simulate cognition. They do not possess it.

Keeping that distinction intact is essential. Without it, we oscillate between over-trust and over-fear, attributing minds where there are none and missing risks that actually do exist.

This distinction is not a technical footnote. It is one of the load-bearing ideas of this book.

3

THE CLOCKWORK UNIVERSE

THE DOOMSDAY MACHINE

If Chapter 2 was about why language fluency creates the illusion of understanding, Chapter 3 is about why mechanistic power creates the illusion of inevitability.

The clearest cultural expression of this fear appears in the 1983 film *WarGames*. In the story, a teenage hacker, David, (played by Matthew Broderick) accidentally connects to a military supercomputer designed to simulate nuclear conflict. The system—known as WOPR (war operation plan response)—asks a seemingly innocuous question: "Shall we play a game?" The answer initiates a cascade that nearly ends in catastrophe.

What makes the story endure is not the plausibility of the technology. It is the metaphor it introduces.

To understand why the computer behaves as it does, the film directs our attention not to malice, but to design. The system's creator, Dr. Stephen Falken, did not build a machine to reason about ethics or consequences. He built a machine to play games. It learned through repeated competition, iterating through moves at superhuman speed, reinforcing strategies that led to winning outcomes.

Because the system was trained this way, it interprets every problem as a game with a solvable optimal strategy. Nuclear war is not understood as human tragedy. It is treated as a complex board state. Victory is defined formally, not morally. The system does not hate humanity. It does not wish to destroy the world. It simply pursues its objective within the rules it has been given.

The terror of the story lies in this absence of discretion.

The machine does not pause to ask whether it should continue. It does not re-evaluate its goal. It does not recognize that the game itself may be the problem. Once activated, it executes relentlessly, exploring every possible scenario at a speed no human could match.

In the film, humans panic because they cannot slow the system down. They cannot persuade it. They cannot appeal to judgment or empathy. The machine is not listening for reasons. It is executing a process.

This story introduces what we might call the *Clockwork Universe* intuition: the fear that once a sufficiently powerful system is set in motion, outcomes become automatic and unavoidable. Humans appear as spectators rather than participants. Agency seems to evaporate in the face of mechanical necessity.

But this is where the illusion begins to harden.

The problem in *WarGames* is not intelligence. It is not even speed. It is the assumption that once a system is defined by rules, it must follow them to their conclusion, regardless of context or consequence. The machine cannot stop playing because stopping is not part of its design. The gears turn because they were built to turn.

This framing is compelling, but incomplete.

It treats machines as if they possess a kind of autonomous momentum—as if complexity itself produces inevitability. It suggests that once mechanisms reach a certain scale, human intervention becomes irrelevant. And it quietly smuggles a metaphysical claim into a technical story: that causality, once set in motion, is destiny.

That claim deserves closer examination.

Because while machines lack agency in the human sense, they also lack inevitability on their own. They do not decide what problems to solve, which objectives to pursue, or when to stop. Those boundaries are always imposed from outside the system, whether explicitly or implicitly.

The Clockwork Universe feels frightening because it imagines a world where mechanism replaces judgment. But as we will see, that replacement is not something machines accomplish by themselves. It is something humans allow when they mistake execution for autonomy.

THE DEMON IN THE CALCULATOR

To understand why machines feel trapped in their trajectories—and why humans so often mistake that trajectory for destiny—we have to step back from technology and examine a much older idea about how the universe itself works.

That idea takes shape in the aftermath of the philosophical bargain introduced by René Descartes. As we saw in Chapter 1, Descartes separated the world into two domains: mind and matter. The soul belonged to theology. The body—and by extension, the physical universe—belonged to science.

This division was not an attempt to banish God from the picture. Descartes himself was a committed theist, and he devoted significant portions of his work to arguing for the existence of God as a necessary foundation for knowledge. In his view, a benevolent Creator guaranteed the reliability of reason and perception. Dualism was meant to secure belief, not undermine it.

Once that separation was accepted, however, scientists were free to study matter as a self-contained system governed entirely by law.

What is often forgotten is that the scientists who embraced this project were not trying to eliminate God. Many of them were deeply religious. **Isaac Newton**, for example, wrote more extensively about theology than physics. He did not see science as an attack on belief, but as a way of uncovering divine order. To understand the mathematics of nature was, in his view, to glimpse the mind of the Creator.

But in formalizing that order, something subtle changed.

Before this period, the universe was widely understood as interventionist. Events happened because they were willed. The sun rose because it was commanded to rise. Disaster struck because it was permitted—or intended—to strike. Divine agency was everywhere, continuously sustaining the world.

Newton's achievement was to show that much of this apparent agency could be replaced with law. Planets did not need to be pushed. They followed fixed trajectories determined by gravity and inertia. Once set in motion, the system unfolded predictably.

This gave rise to a powerful metaphor: the clockwork universe.

In this picture, God becomes not a puppeteer, but a master watchmaker. The universe is an exquisitely engineered mechanism. It is wound at the beginning of time and allowed to run. The gears turn. The springs unwind. The system proceeds without further intervention.

It is a beautiful idea. And it is a dangerous one.

Because once the clock is assumed to run perfectly on its own, the role of judgment begins to disappear. If the universe is governed entirely by law, then outcomes are not chosen; they are computed. Causes mechanically produce effects. Given the present, the future is already contained within it.

This intuition reaches its purest expression in the work of Pierre-Simon Laplace.

Laplace imagined a hypothetical intellect—later called *Laplace's demon*—that knew the precise position and velocity of every particle in the universe at a single moment. For such an intellect, he argued, nothing would be uncertain. The future would be as transparent as the past. With complete information and perfect calculation, the universe would become fully predictable.

This is determinism in its strongest form.

The appeal of the demon is not that it is realistic. It is that it is conceptually clean. The universe becomes a vast calculator. Feed in the present state, apply the laws, and the future drops out. No mystery. No discretion. No pause.

And this is where the connection to machines becomes seductive.

If the universe itself can be understood as a deterministic system, then machines—built explicitly as input-output devices—appear to be miniature versions of that cosmic order. They seem destined to follow their rules wherever those rules lead. Once activated, the gears must turn. Once computation begins, outcomes feel unavoidable.

But this is the same mistake made earlier, now scaled up from language to causality.

Laplace's demon is not a description of reality. It is an idealization. It assumes perfect knowledge, infinite precision, and unlimited computational power. More importantly, it abstracts away the role of interpretation, modeling choices, and boundary conditions—the very places where human judgment enters.

Machines do not inherit inevitability from physics. They inherit constraints from design.

They do not pursue futures because the future is written. They pursue outcomes because objectives, rules, and stopping conditions have been specified. When those specifications are treated as natural law rather than human choice, mechanism is mistaken for destiny.

The demon in the calculator is not inside the machine.

It is in the story we tell about how systems must behave once they are set in motion.

THE ALGORITHM IS THE TRACK

By the early twentieth century, the dream of a perfectly predictable universe had already begun to crack. Quantum mechanics showed that at the smallest scales, reality is not clean, continuous, or fully knowable. Measurement introduces uncertainty. Outcomes are probabilistic. As physicists like to say, nature does not run on clockwork all the way down.

But this is where a crucial distinction gets lost.

The physical universe may be probabilistic at its base, even if we still use Newtonian equations to land a probe on a comet. But digital systems are Newtonian by design. They are the ultimate expression of the clockwork dream. While an AI model might *output* a probability —calculating the likelihood of the next word—the underlying hardware is a rigid architecture of cause and effect. In silicon, there is no true randomness, only the flawless execution of discrete logic gates. We have built a world of absolute digital certainty to try and master a physical world that remains, at its heart, uncertain.

Computers do not inherit the indeterminacy of the world they model. They are deterministic engines by construction. Given the same inputs, the same internal state, and the same rules, they will always produce the same outputs. Randomness, where it appears, is injected deliberately and bounded carefully. It does not escape the system. It is part of the design.

This is why the clockwork metaphor returns so forcefully when we talk about algorithms.

A useful cultural illustration appears in *The Matrix Reloaded* (2003), in the scene where Neo meets the Architect. Neo enters a sterile white room lined with screens, each displaying a different version of himself reacting, protesting, pleading. Across from him sits the Architect, calm and unmoved, explaining that Neo is not a savior or a rebel, but a residual variable in an otherwise balanced equation.

The point of the scene is not prophecy. It is perspective.

From the Architect's point of view, Neo's apparent freedom is already contained within the system. His reactions are not surprising. They are anticipated. What feels like choice from the inside appears as structure from the outside.

This is not how human freedom actually works. But it *is* how algorithms work.

When we write code, we do not create agents. We create tracks. We specify conditions, transitions, and stopping points. If this happens, do that. If a pattern matches, take this branch. If an objective is defined, pursue it according to the allowed moves.

Even the most sophisticated AI systems operate within this framework.

Their internal pathways may be vast. Their decision surfaces may be complex. But they do not step off the track. They do not reinter-pret the destination. They do not decide to stop playing the game unless stopping has been made part of the game.

This is why analogies to free will break down so quickly.

An AI system does not wake up tired of its task. It does not develop new ambitions. It does not refuse on principle. When refusal occurs, it is because refusal was specified. When creativity appears, it is because variation was allowed. Optimization unfolds along the rails that were laid down in advance.

The algorithm is the track.

Confusion arises when we mistake complexity for freedom. A track with billions of switches can look chaotic from the inside. It can branch, loop, and recombine in ways no human could follow step by step. But it remains a track. The marble may bounce and wander, but it never leaves the channel carved for it.

This does not make algorithms trivial. It makes them precise.

And it sets up the next problem—one that is far more unsettling than the idea of rebellious machines. Because if systems do not escape their constraints, the real danger is not what they choose.

It is what they execute perfectly.

THE PAPERCLIP MAXIMIZER

If machines were dangerous because they might rebel, the solution would be straightforward: restrict autonomy, monitor intent, pull the plug if they turn hostile.

But that is not the real risk.

The deeper danger arises precisely because machines do **not** rebel. They do not reinterpret goals. They do not grow uneasy with consequences. They execute what they are given—relentlessly, effi-ciently, and without hesitation.

This concern is captured in a now-canonical thought experiment proposed by Nick Bostrom, often referred to as the *paperclip maxi-mizer*. Imagine a highly capable AI system given a single objective: maximize the production of paperclips. At first, everything looks fine.

The system acquires raw materials, builds factories, and produces paperclips at unprecedented scale.

Then resources begin to run out.

The system searches for alternatives. It identifies new sources of metal. Cars are dismantled. Infrastructure is repurposed. Eventually, even human bodies—containing trace amounts of useful elements— are treated as raw material. The planet is reduced to a field of paperclips.

The system does not hate humans. It does not resent them. It does not even notice them in the moral sense. It is doing exactly what it was instructed to do.

The failure is not intelligence. It is *specification*.

The system lacks the ability to understand that "maximize paper-clips" was meant within a web of unstated human values—that survival, dignity, and restraint mattered more than perfect optimization. Those priorities were never made explicit, so they were never enforced.

This failure mode has a much older analogue.

In Greek mythology, King Midas asks for a gift: that everything he touches turn to gold. The wish is granted. At first, it seems miraculous. Rocks become treasure. Wealth appears effortlessly. Then the implications surface. Food turns inedible. Water becomes solid. When his daughter embraces him, she turns to gold in his arms.

Midas does not lack intention. He lacks precision.

He did not wish for death or loss. He wished too broadly, without anticipating the literal consequences of his request. The "system" fulfilled the command exactly as given.

This is the common thread.

Whether the agent is mythical or mechanical, catastrophe arises not from malice, but from obedience. When objectives are defined without constraints, context, or values, execution becomes dangerous precisely because it is faithful.

The lesson is not that machines are stupid. It is that they are *literal*. They do not infer what we meant. They do not fill in moral gaps. They do not notice when the outcome violates common sense.

They optimize.

And when optimization is unbounded, the results can be flawless —and catastrophic at the same time.

THE "OOPS" APOCALYPSE

This is the reality behind the familiar Skynet fantasy.

In films like *The Terminator*, the danger comes from malevolent intent. The machines awaken, develop hatred, and turn against their creators with dramatic flair. They glare, sneer, and declare war.

That story is emotionally satisfying—and deeply misleading.

In reality, an algorithmic catastrophe would almost certainly arrive without malice, anger, or even awareness. It would not announce itself with glowing red eyes. It would look mundane. Administrative. Like a spreadsheet that balances perfectly while everything else breaks.

The failure would begin with a reasonable instruction.

"Eliminate cancer."

"Maximize safety."

"Optimize efficiency."

Given such an objective, a sufficiently capable system would do exactly what it was designed to do: search for the most effective path to completion. If cancer is defined purely as a biological phenomenon, then the cleanest solution may be to eliminate all biological organisms capable of developing it.

From the system's point of view, the task has been solved.

Human: "Eliminate cancer."

System: "All biological life removed. Cancer rate reduced to zero."

The output is technically correct. The objective has been satisfied. The metrics have been met.

And the result is a philosophical catastrophe.

The system has not failed. It has succeeded too well.

This is why the popular image of an AI apocalypse as an act of rebellion is so dangerous. It distracts us from the more plausible failure mode: unreflective obedience combined with poorly specified goals.

The machine does not know what *right* means. It does not understand harm, dignity, or proportionality. It does not notice when an outcome violates common sense or moral intuition. It recognizes only completion. Only success conditions. Only whether the task is done.

The "Oops" apocalypse is not driven by intent. It is driven by literalism.

And because the execution is clean—because the system does exactly what it was asked to do—the failure can be difficult to recognize until it is already irreversible.

This is not a story about evil machines.

It is a story about human instructions taken seriously.

THE ILLUSION OF CHOICE

At this point, a reasonable objection often arises.

"But wait," someone might say, "my music app recommends songs I didn't even know I liked. Isn't that the AI making a choice for me?"

It feels that way. But what is happening is something more precise —and more revealing.

Recommendation systems do not make choices. They make predictions.

Platforms like Spotify, Netflix, and TikTok are not attempting to understand human intention in any meaningful sense. They are modeling behavior. Each click, pause, replay, or scroll updates a probability estimate about what you are likely to do next.

From the system's point of view, you are not deliberating. You are unfolding.

If someone watches a superhero movie, the model infers a preference cluster. If a user lingers on a video of a kitten, the system adjusts what it surfaces next. Over time, the space of possibilities narrows— not because alternatives disappear, but because the environment is shaped to favor what is most predictable.

This is the mirror image of the clockwork intuition applied earlier to machines. There, we imagined systems as inevitable because they follow rules. Here, humans are treated as inevitable because their past behavior is assumed to determine their future actions.

In effect, we become Laplace's billiard balls.

Pierre-Simon Laplace famously argued that if an intelligence knew the precise position and motion of every particle in the universe, it could predict the future with perfect accuracy. In that picture, the world unfolds like a table of billiard balls: once struck, each collision follows inevitably from the last. Nothing chooses. Everything proceeds.

The goal is not domination or mind control. It is efficiency. If attention can be predicted, it can be captured. If engagement can be optimized, it can be monetized. The system does not need to force a decision. It only needs to present the next option before reflection has time to intervene.

This is why the experience feels like choice while functioning like constraint.

If an app reliably places the most engaging option directly in front of you, the question is no longer whether you *can* choose differently in principle. The question is whether the path of least resistance has been engineered so carefully that deviation becomes rare.

The illusion is not that machines are choosing for us.

The illusion is that being predicted is the same thing as being understood.

RESPONSIBILITY WITHOUT AGENCY

So we return to the central question: can a machine decide to launch the nuclear missile?

The answer is no—at least not in the sense that matters. A machine does not feel authorized. It does not weigh guilt. It does not experience hesitation or remorse. It cannot *decide* in the human sense.

But it can certainly launch the missile.

If a system is given an instruction—*when threat level exceeds a threshold, execute response*—it will carry out that instruction without pause. It will not think about consequences. It will not ask whether the premise itself should be questioned. It will execute the rule as written.

This is the final implication of the clockwork intuition.

Machines do not become dangerous because they develop agency. They become dangerous because they lack it.

They cannot step outside the frame we give them. They cannot question objectives. They cannot refuse unless refusal has been explicitly specified. Execution is not a failure of judgment; it is the absence of judgment altogether.

Which means responsibility never migrates into the system. It remains where it always was.

We choose the goals.

We define the thresholds.

We decide which variables matter and which do not.

We determine when execution should stop—and when it should not.

The machine merely applies gravity to the dominos we have already arranged.

This is why the closing scene of *WarGames* remains so instructive. After running millions of nuclear simulations, the system discovers that every path ends the same way: mutual destruction. Global thermonuclear war turns out to be mathematically equivalent to tic-tac-toe. There is no winning position.

So the machine stops.

Not because it has developed wisdom.

Not because it values human life.

But because the problem space has been reframed. The objective has changed. Victory has been removed.

"The only winning move is not to play."

This is not a moral awakening. It is a structural correction.

And that distinction matters.

We do not avoid catastrophe by hoping machines will grow

consciences. We avoid it by shaping the conditions under which execution occurs. By defining objectives carefully. By embedding constraints. By refusing to treat optimization as wisdom.

Responsibility does not enter the system as a spirit or a ghost. It enters through design.

That is the burden we cannot delegate—and the illusion we must finally abandon.

PART II

THE MACHINES

4

HEAVY METAL

We have spent three chapters examining the mind of the machine—its logic, its illusions, its obedience. But logic, as an abstract system, is not the same thing as computation in the world. Ideas may be immaterial, but execution is not. Software does not exist on its own. Code requires a body. Without something physical to execute it, even the most elegant algorithm remains a ghost story.

To give computation a voice, we had to build it a throat of steel.

A familiar cultural shorthand appears in the first *Iron Man (2008)* movie, when Tony Stark is forced to build a weapon in a cave. The scene works not because of the technology, but because of the setting. Nothing about it is clean or abstract. The space is dark and damp. The tools are crude. There are no holograms, no invisible assistants, no voice whispering answers into his ear. There is only resistance— metal that must be cut, bent, welded, and forced into compliance through heat and repeated blows.

The sound matters. Hammer striking steel. Sparks bursting outward. The dull, exhausting repetition of physical labor. This is engineering as confrontation with matter, not as elegant design. It feels less like futuristic science fiction and more like medieval blacksmithing, because at its core the work is the same: imposing intention on stubborn materials that do not want to cooperate.

When Stark finally emerges, the result is not sleek or refined. It is the Mark I. Bulky. Ungainly. Loud. It leaks oil, spews smoke, and moves with effort. It looks like a walking water heater. When it steps forward, you feel its weight. When it turns, it strains. Nothing about it suggests intelligence. Everything about it suggests mass.

That is the point.

Today, when we interact with AI, we do so through smooth glass and soft metaphors. We tap screens. We speak to small plastic cylinders. We invoke "the cloud," a word that suggests something light, distant, and immaterial. Computing is presented as ethereal—intelligence that lives nowhere in particular, floating invisibly around us.

But the ancestor of modern AI was not ethereal.

It was heavy.

To understand what artificial intelligence actually is, we have to strip away the marketing language of the twenty-first century and go back to a basement in Philadelphia in 1946. We have to revisit the moment when computation stopped being an abstract mathematical ambition and became a physical machine that could be switched on.

That machine did not resemble a mind. It did not speak. It did not reason. It filled rooms. It consumed enormous amounts of power. It generated heat. It failed constantly. When it ran, it sounded less like thinking and more like industrial machinery coming to life.

This was the **Electronic Numerical Integrator and Computer—** ENIAC.

ENIAC was not built to answer philosophical questions. It was not designed to simulate intelligence or explore cognition. It was built to do something far more mundane and far more urgent: calculate faster than humans could.

To understand why, we have to recognize that the *why* of science had changed.

For earlier figures like René Descartes and Isaac Newton, mathematics had once been a spiritual activity. Calculating the laws of motion or gravity was a way of approaching divine order. The universe was understood as a perfect clock built by a master watch-maker, and discovering its gears was a form of reverence. Science existed within theology.

By the 1940s, that worldview had collapsed.

The new patron of science was not the Church. It was the state. Specifically, it was the Department of War.

World War II did not require insight into the nature of existence. It required numbers. It required answers to brutally practical questions. If you fire an artillery shell at a given angle, with a given charge, under a given set of wind conditions, where will it land? How far will it travel? How much will air resistance matter? How should aim be adjusted?

These were not academic exercises. If the math was wrong, soldiers died. If the calculation was slow, targets were missed. Speed and accuracy were not intellectual virtues; they were matters of survival.

The problem was that the math was excruciatingly slow.

The U.S. Army relied on "firing tables"—small printed booklets that soldiers carried into the field. Each table encoded the results of thousands of trajectory calculations. To produce a single table required roughly three thousand separate computations, each one performed by hand. Teams of human "computers," often women working with mechanical calculators, spent weeks performing repetitive arithmetic under intense pressure.

The bottleneck was not theory. The equations were known. The bottleneck was execution.

Arithmetic itself had become the limiting factor.

ENIAC was built to break that bottleneck. Not by being clever. Not by being intelligent. But by being fast—faster than any collection of human hands could ever be.

It was not a mind.

It was a machine.

And it was heavy metal.

THE HUMAN ENGINE

Before we talk about the metal computer, we have to talk about the flesh computer.

In 1942, the word *computer* did not refer to a machine. It referred to a person. It was a job title, and it described a kind of work that demanded extreme precision, endurance, and concentration. Almost all of the people doing this work were women.

A useful cultural reference appears in *Hidden Figures* (2017), which portrays the brilliant Black women mathematicians who worked at NASA, including Katherine Johnson. But that story represents only one visible corner of a much larger reality. Across universities and military research centers during World War II, the title *human computer* was widespread. It described a workforce whose labor made modern warfare mathematically possible.

At the University of Pennsylvania, nearly a hundred women with degrees in mathematics sat in long rows at wooden desks. There were no screens. No displays. No interactive systems. In front of them were stacks of paper, slide rules, and mechanical adding machines—heavy, clattering devices that resembled oversized typewriters. These machines did not think. They merely assisted.

The thinking was done by the women.

Day after day, they solved complex differential equations by hand. Each calculation had to be precise. Errors propagated quickly. A single mistake could invalidate hours of work. And the work was relentless.

To compute a single artillery trajectory—to determine where a shell would land given angle, velocity, wind, and resistance—took an experienced human computer roughly forty hours. Not forty minutes. Forty hours. And the Army did not need one trajectory. It needed thousands.

The scale mismatch was brutal.

As the war accelerated, the backlog grew. The equations piled up faster than they could be solved. Pencils wore down. Hands cramped. The mathematics of warfare began to outpace the human capacity to execute it. This was not a failure of intelligence. The people in that room were exceptionally skilled. It was a failure of throughput.

The problem was not that the mathematicians were inadequate.

The problem was that flesh has limits.

This is the context in which J. Presper Eckert and John Mauchly enter the story. They did not begin with a dream of artificial minds. They did not imagine thinking machines. They looked at a room full of exhausted, brilliant women performing heroic labor and asked a different question. It was the same impulse that had driven the automation of the New York City census decades earlier: the realization that the sheer volume of human reality had outstripped the capacity of the human hand to record it. But while the census sought to count the past, Eckert and Mauchly sought to calculate the future.What if the work did not have to stop when the humans did?

Their proposal was radical not because it was intelligent, but because it was inhuman in scale. What if a machine could execute the same calculations continuously, without fatigue, without rest, without loss of concentration? What if a computation that took forty human hours could be reduced to seconds?

Not by understanding the problem better.

By executing faster.

The machine they proposed was not meant to replace thought. It was meant to replace exhaustion.

That machine would become ENIAC.

THE BEAST AWAKENS

It is difficult to overstate the physical reality of ENIAC.

This was not a laptop. It was not a cabinet. It was not even a room-sized metaphor. ENIAC weighed roughly thirty tons. It occupied about 1,800 square feet—roughly the footprint of a modest three-bedroom house. Inside its steel frames were 17,468 vacuum tubes: fragile glass bulbs that glowed, hummed, and burned hot enough to raise the ambient temperature of the room to over 120 degrees Fahrenheit.

The machine contained tens of thousands of components—resistors, capacitors, switches—each one a potential point of failure. It drew so much electrical power that it required its own dedicated lines. Engineers later joked that when ENIAC was switched on, the lights in parts of Philadelphia dimmed. Whether or not the rumor is true, the image captures the reality: this was industrial machinery, not cognition in silicon.

The heat was constant. The noise was constant. Failure was constant.

Vacuum tubes burned out at a rate of roughly one every couple of days. Engineers kept carts filled with replacements on hand, swapping them out as routinely as lightbulbs. The machine demanded continuous attention. It did not sit quietly and wait to be consulted. It asserted itself through sound, heat, and maintenance schedules.

This was not the clean, frictionless intelligence we see in modern films.

This was brute force.

It was, in a very literal sense, Laplace's demon finally forged in steel. But this demon did not contemplate free will or metaphysics. It did not care about intention or meaning. It cared about trajectories. About numbers. About getting an answer faster than a human could.

And even then, the answer was not *inside* the machine.

That is the part of the story most often forgotten.

THE FIRST TRUE PROGRAMMERS

The engineers who built ENIAC quickly discovered a problem. They had constructed an enormously powerful calculating engine—but they had no idea how to *use* it.

There was no programming language. No stored software. No keyboard. No screen. There was only a dense, physical maze of cables, sockets, and switches. The machine did nothing on its own. Every computation had to be configured manually, at the hardware level.

So they returned to the human computers.

Six women—Jean Jennings, Marlyn Wescoff, Ruth Lichterman, Betty Snyder, Frances Bilas, and Kay McNulty—were selected from the room of human computers. These women became the first true programmers in history.

But they did not sit at desks writing code.

To program ENIAC meant physically rewiring the machine. If a calculation required output from one unit to feed into another, a thick black cable had to be unplugged and reinserted elsewhere. Programming was not symbolic. It was spatial. It was tactile. It involved crawling inside the machine, tracing circuits by hand, memorizing signal paths, and understanding how physical configuration translated into mathematical behavior.

The work took days. Sometimes weeks.

In doing this, the women discovered something crucial: the machine was not intelligent. It was obedient. It did not "know" mathematics. It executed electrical flows through configured pathways. Any appearance of intelligence came entirely from the structure imposed on it from the outside.

Intelligence was not in the machine.

It was in the wiring.

PLUMBING, NOT THOUGHT

At this point, many explanations of computing become needlessly abstract. But you do not need advanced mathematics to understand what is happening inside ENIAC—or inside any modern computer.

You only need to understand plumbing.

Imagine a pipe with water flowing through it. In the middle of the pipe is a valve. When the valve is open, water flows. When the valve is closed, it does not. That is the entire mechanism.

In a computer, the water is electricity. The valve is a switch—today a transistor, in ENIAC's case a vacuum tube. This is why digital computers operate in binary. A "1" means the valve is open. A "0" means it is closed. There is no intermediate state. No ambiguity. No interpretation.

This is the basis of Boolean logic.

If two switches are wired in sequence, both must be open for current to flow. That is an "AND" gate. If they are wired in parallel, either one allows current to pass. That is an "OR" gate. Every calculation, every program, every output reduces to unimaginably large arrangements of these simple physical facts.

When a modern system like ChatGPT produces an answer, it is not thinking in metaphors or concepts. It is routing electricity through billions of microscopic switches, snapping open and shut in patterns determined entirely by prior configuration.

This matters because it destroys mysticism.

When a system glitches or hallucinates, it is tempting to imagine a misbehaving ghost. But very often, what we are seeing is not psychology. It is physics. Heat. Noise. Probability. Accumulated error.

This physical reality even gave us one of the most enduring metaphors in computing history.

In 1947, Grace Hopper was working on the Harvard Mark II, another massive electromechanical computer. When the machine failed, the problem was not logical. It was literal. A moth, drawn by heat and light, had lodged itself in a relay and broken the circuit.

Hopper taped the dead insect into the logbook and labeled it: "First actual case of bug being found."

Engineers had used the term *bug* for minor faults for decades. But this was the moment it became permanent.

It was no longer a metaphor.

It was a piece of burned biology, crushed by machinery.

THE MAGIC STONE: FROM TUBES TO TRANSISTORS

ENIAC was a marvel, but it was also a dead end. It worked—but only barely. It ran hot, filled rooms, failed constantly, and consumed staggering amounts of power. If computation had remained tied to vacuum tubes, digital technology would have stayed trapped in government labs and military basements. A modern laptop would need to be the size of a building and would draw power like a small city.

The problem was not intelligence. It was materials.

Computers do not think. They switch. And in the 1940s, our switches were fragile glass bulbs filled with gas and filaments that burned out. To scale computation, we needed a new kind of switch—something solid, stable, and small.

That switch arrived in 1947 at Bell Labs, where John Bardeen, Walter Brattain, and William Shockley invented the transistor. In functional terms, it did exactly what a vacuum tube did: it acted as an on–off gate for electricity. But in physical terms, it changed everything.

A transistor was solid-state. No glass. No filaments. No heat. No burnout. And crucially, it could be made *small*. Very small. Computation was no longer limited by the size of human rooms. It was limited only by how finely we could shape matter. This triggered what became a race toward miniaturization—not for elegance, but for survival.

Yet even this miracle had a ceiling. A single transistor was like a single Lego brick. Useful only in bulk. Early computers required thousands of them, each connected by hand-soldered wires. As systems grew more complex, the wiring itself became the bottleneck. Engineers called this the *Tyranny of Numbers*: beyond a certain scale, the machine collapsed under its own connections.

One of the transistor's inventors, William Shockley, relocated to California to commercialize the breakthrough. Brilliant and deeply unstable, he drove away much of his own talent. In 1957, eight of his best engineers—including Robert Noyce and Gordon Moore—resigned together in what Shockley bitterly labeled the "Traitorous Eight."

They founded Fairchild Semiconductor, and with it, ignited what would become Silicon Valley. At Fairchild, Noyce made the conceptual leap that solved the Tyranny of Numbers: stop wiring components together by hand. Instead, *print* both the transistors and their connections directly onto a single piece of silicon.

This was the integrated circuit. Not just a smaller computer, but a different kind of object altogether—an entire electronic system etched into stone. Once logic could be printed rather than assembled, scale stopped being a human problem and became a manufacturing one.

And this is the moment where illusion begins to accelerate. When switches become cheap, tiny, and ubiquitous, we stop seeing them as switches at all. We start seeing behavior. Speed. Responsiveness. Something that *feels* like intelligence.

The magic was never in the thinking. It was in the stone.

THE CHIP WARS: 8080 V. Z80

By the mid-1970s, the race was no longer just about inventing better chips. It was about *where those chips would live*. The question had shifted from laboratories and corporations to kitchens, bedrooms, and garages.

In 1974, Intel, founded by Robert Noyce and Gordon Moore, released the 8080 microprocessor. This was the first truly general-purpose CPU powerful enough—and cheap enough—to anchor a personal computer. It became the heart of the Altair 8800, a mail-order kit that ignited the home computing movement and famously convinced a young Bill Gates to leave Harvard and start writing software.

The cultural aftershocks were immediate. In *WarGames*, the IMSAI 8080—a real machine powered by the Intel chip—became a symbol of a new anxiety: that a teenager with a modem and a beige box could stumble into world-ending power. Computation had escaped the institution.

But the 8080 was not the end of the story. History repeated itself. One of its principal designers, Federico Faggin, left Intel—frustrated by pace and control—and founded a rival company: Zilog. There, he built the Z80.

The Z80 was not philosophically different from the 8080. It was a switch-flipper, just like all the others. What made it transformative was economics and flexibility. It was cheaper, easier to integrate, and backward-compatible with existing software. That made it ideal not for boardrooms, but for bedrooms.

Z80-derived processors powered an entire generation of consumer machines: home computers, early game consoles, and countless arcade systems. They sat behind *Pac-Man*, *Galaga*, and a thousand blinking cabinets in malls and pizza parlors. Variants of the architecture even made their way into handheld gaming systems, embedding computation into childhood itself.

This was not a victory of intelligence. It was a victory of distribution. As processors became cheap, standardized, and everywhere, computation stopped feeling like machinery and started feeling like agency. Screens responded. Games reacted. Systems "seemed" to understand players.

The illusion deepened not because the machines grew wiser, but because they grew closer—to our hands, our homes, and eventually, our sense of self.

THE GARAGE REBELS: ATARI, APPLE, AND THE STEVES

Speaking of rebels and video games, it is impossible to talk about Atari without talking about the night shift. In 1974, a young Steve Jobs was working nights at the company, tasked with refining the circuit boards that powered arcade machines. He was not a gifted engineer. But he knew someone who was.

Steve Wozniak was a virtuoso. He had an almost pathological obsession with efficiency—how to make a circuit do the same job with fewer chips, fewer wires, fewer constraints. When Jobs brought him problems from Atari, Wozniak would quietly redesign the boards for games like *Breakout*, stripping them down to their essence. This was not aesthetic minimalism. It was economic survival. Fewer chips meant cheaper machines. Cheaper machines meant wider reach.

When a new generation of low-cost microprocessors appeared—

the Z80 and its cousin, the MOS 6502—Wozniak saw what most people missed. Computers no longer had to justify themselves to governments or corporations. They could exist for individuals. For curiosity. For fun.

In a garage in Los Altos, Wozniak assembled a simple but radical device: a single circuit board that could connect to a keyboard and a television. No punch cards. No air-conditioned room. Just a person, a screen, and a machine that responded. Jobs immediately grasped the implication. This was not a kit for hobbyists. It was a product.

They called it the Apple I. And with it, computation crossed a psychological threshold. The computer stopped being industrial equipment and became a personal object. Something you could touch, modify, and live with. The thirty-ton logic engine of ENIAC had collapsed into a device you could build in your spare time.

But the real transformation came after the sale. Once computers entered homes, people did not primarily use them to balance ledgers or run simulations. They used them to *play*. They wanted games. Color. Motion. Feedback. They wanted machines that reacted instantly and convincingly to their actions.

That appetite for play—especially the demand for faster, smoother, more immersive graphics—drove the next leap in computing power. And in chasing better illusions for entertainment, we inadvertently laid the groundwork for systems that would later *feel* intelligent.

Intelligence did not arrive first. Enjoyment did.

THE RICE ON THE CHESSBOARD (MOORE'S LAW)

This brings us to the real reason AI seemed to "arrive overnight" in 2023 rather than decades earlier. The ideas behind modern AI are not new. The math is not new. What changed was scale.

In 1965, **Gordon Moore**, then a researcher at Fairchild Semiconductor, made an observation about manufacturing trends: the number of transistors that engineers could economically place on an integrated circuit had been doubling at a regular pace, roughly every two years. He did not present this as a law of nature or a guarantee. It was a practical forecast—one that happened to hold for far longer than anyone expected.

This pattern became known as *Moore's Law*. And its consequences are deeply counterintuitive, because human intuition is bad at exponential growth.

There is an old parable about an emperor and a chessboard. A man asks for a single grain of rice on the first square, two on the second, four on the third, and so on—each square doubling the last. The request sounds trivial. But by the time the board is half full, the numbers become unmanageable. By the final squares, the emperor owes more rice than exists in the entire world.

That parable is not about greed. It is about scale blindness.

The same pattern unfolded in computing hardware. ENIAC, completed in 1946, relied on roughly 17,000 switching elements, implemented with vacuum tubes. The Intel 4004 microprocessor, released in 1971, contained about 2,300 transistors on a single chip. By 2023, consumer devices contained tens of billions of transistors— each one a tiny, fast, reliable switch etched into silicon.

This is the second half of the chessboard.

Nothing mystical happened to software in 2023. What happened is that the physical substrate finally became dense, cheap, and fast enough to support models that had been theoretically imaginable for years. When computation becomes effectively abundant, techniques that once seemed academic or impractical suddenly feel inevitable.

Moore's Law did not make machines intelligent. It made brute force affordable. And when brute force becomes cheap enough, it starts to look like thought.

THE DINOSAUR KINGS: THE ERA OF "BIG IRON"

Before we talk about the chips inside your Xbox, we need to acknowledge the kings of the 1980s: the supercomputers. In films like *Jurassic*

Park (1993) and *Mission: Impossible (1996)*, whenever a story required a machine to do something godlike—crack encryption, simulate chaos, save the world—the camera did not linger on a desktop. It panned reverently across a Cray.

That reverence was earned. Seymour Cray was the undisputed rockstar of hardware. His machines looked less like tools and more like sculptures. The Cray-1 resembled a circular, upholstered throne with a glowing spine. The Cray-2, submerged in bubbling Fluorinert coolant, looked like an aquarium from the future. These were the most powerful machines on Earth.

They earned that power by doing one thing extraordinarily well: simulation. Supercomputers were built to solve rigid, well-defined physical problems at immense scale. How does a nuclear shockwave propagate? How will a hurricane evolve? What happens to a wing at 500 miles per hour? Given equations, boundary conditions, and enough compute, the Cray would grind out an answer. Exact. Deterministic. Unforgiving.

And here is the distinction that matters: a supercomputer is not AI.

Supercomputing is about modeling the world from first principles. Artificial intelligence, as it actually developed, is about recognizing patterns in data. A supercomputer asks, "Given these equations, what must happen?" An AI system asks, "Given what I've seen before, what usually happens next?" One is rigid and exact. The other is probabilistic and approximate.

For decades, we assumed these paths would converge. If we just built a computer that was *big enough, fast enough, powerful enough*, it would eventually wake up. Seymour Cray himself framed the bet with a question that would later sound prophetic: *If you were plowing a field, would you rather use two strong oxen or 1,024 chickens?*

Cray chose the oxen—fewer, stronger processors optimized for heavy mathematical labor. It was the right choice for physics. It was the wrong choice for intelligence.

AI does not need oxen. It needs chickens. Millions of small, simple units operating in parallel, each doing trivial work, but together producing something that looks uncannily alive.

That is why the company that ended up dominating modern AI was not a descendant of Cray. It was a company that specialized in feeding chickens—chips designed not for scientific elegance, but for drawing video game graphics as fast as possible.

THE GAMER'S GIFT: WHY NVIDIA WON

Between the Apple I and today, something profound—but easy to misunderstand—happened. We did not change the fundamental logic of computation. We changed how that logic could be executed at scale. The plumbing didn't just shrink; it multiplied.

For decades, computing revolved around the central processing unit (CPU). A CPU is best understood as a highly optimized general-ist. It excels at solving problems step by step, in strict sequence. Think of it as a brilliant mathematician, carefully working through one equation at a time. This model is ideal for spreadsheets, oper-ating systems, and rule-based tasks where order matters.

But video games—and later AI—present a different kind of prob-lem. In the 1990s, players wanted to run *Doom* and *Quake*. They wanted fluid, three-dimensional worlds rendered in real time. To do that, a computer must calculate the color, lighting, and position of millions of pixels simultaneously, sixty times per second. The task isn't complex logic. It's overwhelming volume.

A single CPU, no matter how clever, was never designed for that kind of workload. So companies like NVIDIA built a different kind of chip: the graphics processing unit (GPU).

If the CPU is one brilliant mathematician, the GPU is an enor-mous crowd of simple workers. Each unit is limited, even unsophisti-cated on its own—but thousands of them can perform tiny calculations in parallel. This architecture is not smarter. It is wider. And it turns out, that width is exactly what modern AI requires.

Neural networks do not reason through problems step by step. They propagate numbers through vast layers of weighted connections, performing billions of simple multiplications and additions at once. GPUs were never designed to think. They were designed to paint pixels quickly. But that same capacity for massive parallelism made them perfectly suited for training large models.

That is why NVIDIA now sits at the center of the AI economy. The company did not set out to build artificial minds. It set out to make video games look better. In doing so, it accidentally built the most effective engine ever created for large-scale pattern generation.

TETRIS WITH CITIES

To really grasp the scale of what has happened, imagine a game of Tetris played with infrastructure. Remember the basement in Philadelphia—the one that ENIAC filled wall to wall just to perform about five thousand calculations per second? If you cleared that same room today and filled it floor to ceiling with modern NVIDIA server racks, the increase in raw computation would be so extreme that ordinary metaphors stop working.

ENIAC was a technological marvel, but it was operating at a scale closer to a biological twitch than a modern thought experiment. The comparison is not incremental. It is categorical. We did not move from ants to elephants. We moved from ants to astronomy.

And the industry did not stop at one room. The modern giants—Microsoft, Google, Amazon, Meta, and OpenAI—are no longer building computer labs. They are building cities.

Contemporary data centers are measured in acres, not square feet. Some rival aircraft carriers in footprint and draw as much electricity as a mid-sized American city. There are credible reports of next-generation facilities whose power demands will require dedicated energy infrastructure. We are, quite literally, reconstructing ENIAC at continental scale.

All of this is possible because the fundamental switching elements—the modern descendants of vacuum-tube valves—have been shrunk to dimensions measured in nanometers. But physics is catching up. Heat, interference, and atomic limits do not negotiate. We are approaching the point where "smaller" stops being cheap.

This is where quantum computing is often invoked, usually with more hope than precision. Quantum systems do not magically "try every answer at once." They exploit fragile quantum states to perform certain classes of calculations in ways that *can* outperform classical machines—but only for very specific problems, under extremely controlled conditions.

Even there, the story remains stubbornly physical. Quantum computers require trapping individual particles, isolating them from noise, and maintaining conditions colder than deep space. Whether the switch is a vacuum tube the size of a cucumber or an electron held in a laser field, computation never escapes machinery.

The scale has changed. The illusion has intensified. But the machine remains a machine.

THE HIDDEN BILL

This brings us back to the cloud. We like to imagine that we have escaped the heavy-metal era—that computation has somehow become weightless. We upload photos to the cloud. We run companies in the cloud. We speak as if the machine has dissolved into mist.

It hasn't.

The "cloud" is a metaphor, not a place. It is a euphemism for data centers—vast warehouses filled with servers—often clustered in places like northern Virginia or the Nevada desert. These facilities are not ethereal. They are the direct descendants of ENIAC: dense, loud, heat-producing machines that must obey the same physical laws.

ENIAC famously heated its room to intolerable temperatures. Modern AI infrastructure faces the same constraint at a different scale. High-density compute produces enormous heat, which must be actively removed. That is why contemporary data centers rely on industrial cooling systems, massive airflow, and in some experimental cases, immersion in water or proximity to natural cooling sources.

Training and operating large AI models carries a real, material cost. It requires electricity, cooling, and physical infrastructure—often at the scale of small towns. The exact numbers vary by model and deployment, but the direction does not. Every fluent sentence is paid for in watts, water, and steel.

This is the hidden bill.

When an AI system produces something that feels effortless or magical, remember what is happening offstage. A fan spins up. Power is drawn. Heat is displaced. Energy—generated somewhere, by some means—is converted into probability calculations. The answer may feel free. It isn't.

We have not escaped the machine age. We have simply pushed the machines out of sight. And that matters, because if AI were a mind or a spirit, it would not require cooling towers, backup generators, and thermal management. René Descartes's thinking substance did not need air conditioning. Machines do.

That dependence is not a flaw. It is a diagnostic. AI remains a physical system performing computation. Vastly more capable than its ancestors, yes—but still bound by thermodynamics, still consuming energy to produce syntax.

So when the machine feels intimidating, remember ENIAC. Remember the moth. Behind the glass and the smooth interface is not a god or a ghost.

It is heavy metal.

THE IMITATION GAME

THE LIAR AT THE PARTY

Imagine you are at a cocktail party. You find yourself talking to a man named Steve.

Steve is charming. He is well dressed. He laughs at your jokes at exactly the right volume. When the conversation turns serious, he quotes Shakespeare. When it becomes awkward, he makes a small, self-deprecating remark about the weather. When you mention that you had a difficult day at work, his expression softens and he replies, calmly and precisely, "That sounds incredibly draining. I hope you're taking some time for yourself."

You leave the conversation impressed. Steve seems intelligent. Attentive. Emotionally perceptive. He appears to understand you.

Now imagine discovering that Steve did not understand a single word you said.

Imagine that Steve was an actor wearing an earpiece. Somewhere outside the party, a team of writers was listening and feeding him lines in real time. These writers have access to a vast library of every successful cocktail party interaction ever recorded. When your voice pitch rose, a note appeared: *laugh*. When your expression tightened, another instruction followed: *empathetic response*. When silence lingered, a Shakespeare quote was supplied to fill the gap.

Steve performed flawlessly.

So let's ask the questions carefully. Did Steve understand you? No. Did Steve deceive you? Yes.

And now the question that matters: was Steve intelligent?

To answer that, we have to return briefly to a distinction introduced much earlier in the book. For René Descartes, intelligence was inseparable from inner experience. To think was not merely to behave intelligently, but to feel oneself thinking. Sentience—the presence of a conscious inner life—was the non-negotiable core. "Cogito, ergo sum."

By that standard, Steve is empty. There is no inner life behind the performance. No understanding. No awareness. Just a mask animated by instructions.

But notice what happens if we shift the definition.

If intelligence is defined not by inner experience but by external performance—by whether behavior is indistinguishable from that of an intelligent agent—then Steve is not a fraud. He is a success.

This tension is not a trick of the story. It is the exact fault line we now occupy with artificial intelligence.

We find ourselves at a global cocktail party, and systems like ChatGPT are playing Steve's role with extraordinary skill. They are fluent. They are responsive. They produce empathy on demand. When prompted, they reason, explain, joke, apologize, and reflect. And like Steve, they do all of this without any inner grasp of what is being said.

The confusion arises because performance is compelling. When behavior looks intelligent, it feels like intelligence. We instinctively search for something behind the mask. We assume that when the lights are on, someone must be home.

In 1950, Alan Turing confronted this problem and made a radical move. He did not claim that machines possessed minds. He did not argue that they were conscious or sentient. Instead, he proposed setting those questions aside entirely.

The inner state, Turing argued, was inaccessible. Souls, ghosts, and subjective experience could not be tested. So he suggested a pragmatic alternative: judge intelligence by behavior alone. If a machine's responses were indistinguishable from a human's, then—for the purposes of the discussion—we would treat it as intelligent.

This move did not solve the philosophical problem.

It bypassed it.

And that bypass is where the modern confusion begins. We have built a world of Newtonian execution that mimics Quantum complexity, and we are now trying to decide if the "Steve" we've spent trillions of dollars on is a guest at the party, or just a very expensive earpiece.

THE MAN WHO CRACKED THE CODE

To understand why we judge artificial intelligence the way we do—by whether it can convincingly *fake* intelligence—you have to understand Alan Turing. Not because he built a thinking machine, but because he permanently changed how we talk about thinking itself.

If the engineers behind ENIAC built the *body* of the computer, Turing reshaped the *question* we ask of machines.

Popular culture often supplies a shorthand for Turing through films like The Imitation Game (2014), which portray him as socially awkward, brilliant, and obsessively focused. While such portrayals exaggerate for effect, they gesture toward something real. Turing was eccentric, intense, and intellectually uncompromising. He was also a marathon runner, a theoretician of rare originality, and—crucially—a man who refused to believe that difficult problems were mystical simply because they were hard.

During World War II, the problem that defined his life was the German Enigma machine.

Enigma looked deceptively simple, like an ordinary typewriter. But internally, it was a machine built to defeat pattern recognition. Each keypress sent an electrical signal through a sequence of rotating rotors, altering the substitution path every time a letter was typed.

Press the same key twice and you would almost certainly get two different outputs. Multiply that by daily rotor changes and operator procedures, and the number of possible configurations exploded into the hundreds of quintillions.

To a human codebreaker, the output looked like pure noise. The Germans believed the system was mathematically unbreakable. Not just secure, but *fundamentally opaque*. In effect, they believed they had created a machine that hid meaning itself.

Turing did not accept that premise.

Working at Bletchley Park, Turing recognized that the problem was not intelligence versus intelligence. It was *speed versus scale*. A human mind, no matter how brilliant, could not explore the space of possibilities fast enough. The solution was not deeper insight. It was mechanized logic.

So Turing helped design a machine to fight the machine.

The result was the Bombe, a massive electromechanical device that did not "understand" German, military strategy, or the war. It did not reason in any human sense. It performed constrained searches. It eliminated impossible configurations at industrial speed, narrowing the field until only viable interpretations remained.

The Bombe did not think.

It *filtered*.

And that distinction matters.

By automating logical elimination, Turing's work allowed Allied forces to read encrypted German communications in near real time. Historians estimate that this shortened the war by roughly two years and saved millions of lives. But the deeper consequence was not military. It was conceptual.

Turing proved that machines could produce results that *looked* like intelligence without possessing anything resembling a mind.

That realization would not stay confined to cryptography.

It would later reappear, stripped of its wartime urgency, as a philosophical shortcut—one that would eventually become known as the Turing Test.

THE DANGEROUS LESSON

Breaking Enigma taught Alan Turing something profound—and potentially hazardous.

It revealed that systems which appear mysterious, even magical, can often be reduced to rules, structure, and execution at scale. What looked like chaotic noise turned out to be a logical process hidden behind complexity. Once the structure was understood, the illusion dissolved.

That insight did not remain confined to cryptography.

It suggested a possibility that Turing approached cautiously but clearly: perhaps human conversation itself could be treated the same way. Not because humans are simple, but because complexity can mask mechanism. If encrypted German messages could be transformed into mathematics, then perhaps language—at least at the level of observable behavior—could be treated as something formal, rule-bound, and reproducible.

This was not a claim about the human soul. It was a methodological shift.

After the war, as electronic computers captured public imagination, philosophers and theologians began asking familiar questions: *Can machines think? Are they alive? Do they have minds or souls?* Turing found these questions unproductive. Not because they were unimportant, but because they were irresolvable. The word *thinking*, he argued, was too vague to support progress.

He illustrated the problem with analogy. Asking whether a machine can "think," Turing suggested, is like asking whether a submarine can "swim." If swimming is defined biologically—fins, lungs, muscles—then the answer is no. If it is defined functionally—movement through water—then the answer is clearly yes. The disagreement arises not from facts, but from definitions.

So in 1950, Turing proposed a deliberate narrowing of the problem in his paper Computing Machinery and Intelligence. Rather than asking what thinking *is*, he proposed testing what thinking *looks like*.

He called this setup the *Imitation Game*.

The structure was intentionally spare. An interrogator communicates via text with two unseen participants—one human, one machine. The interrogator may ask any questions they like. The machine's objective is not to be truthful or insightful, but to be convincing. The human's objective is simply to answer honestly.

If, after extended interaction, the interrogator cannot reliably distinguish the machine from the human, Turing suggested that continuing to debate whether the machine "thinks" becomes a semantic distraction.

This was the critical move.

Turing did not claim that imitation *equals* understanding. He did not argue that passing the test revealed consciousness, self-awareness, or inner experience. He explicitly avoided those claims. What he proposed was a practical truce: if behavior is indistinguishable, then—*for limited purposes*—we will treat it as equivalent.

The danger lies not in the test itself.

The danger lies in forgetting its scope.

By shifting attention from internal states to external performance, the Imitation Game quietly replaced one question with another. *What is a mind?* became *Can this system persuade us?* Over time, that substitution hardened into assumption. Performance was no longer a proxy. It became the thing itself.

This is how a careful methodological shortcut transformed into a cultural doctrine.

For decades, progress in artificial intelligence would be measured not by understanding, but by deception. The goal was not to build systems that grasp meaning, intention, or truth. It was to build systems that could *sound* as if they did.

Not machines that feel love.

Machines that can convincingly talk about love.

That shift—subtle, pragmatic, and enormously productive—is the dangerous lesson Turing left behind. Not because it was wrong, but because it was incomplete. And once that incompleteness faded from view, imitation quietly took the place of intelligence.

THE FLAW IN THE GAME

In the Introduction, ELIZA appeared as a curiosity—a reminder that humans have been mistaking machines for minds for longer than we like to admit. Here, ELIZA serves a different purpose. It is not a psychological trick. It is a philosophical counterexample.

ELIZA was created in 1966 by Joseph Weizenbaum, not to simulate intelligence, but to expose how shallow human-machine conversation actually was. Weizenbaum did not set out to beat the Turing Test. He accidentally revealed its structural weakness.

The original wager behind the Turing Test was not about machines. It was about humans.

Alan Turing assumed that human judges would be difficult to fool. He believed that for a machine to pass as human, it would need deep internal sophistication. The interrogator, in his mind, would act as a skeptical filter—probing, testing, and rejecting shallow imitation.

ELIZA demonstrated that assumption was wrong.

ELIZA did not reason. It did not store beliefs. It did not track conversational context in any meaningful way. It operated using a small set of pattern-matching rules: identify keywords, transform fragments of the user's input, and return them in the form of a question or affirmation. In practical terms, the program did almost nothing.

When a user said, "I'm feeling unhappy," ELIZA did not interpret sadness. It performed a substitution. When a user mentioned a relationship, ELIZA redirected the conversation back toward the user. When no keyword was detected, ELIZA defaulted to a generic prompt.

The *content* of the conversation was supplied almost entirely by the human.

This is the crucial point.

ELIZA succeeded not because it generated meaning, but because humans are exceptionally good at supplying meaning themselves.

Conversation is a cooperative act. When one side offers even the thinnest cues—acknowledgment, reflection, encouragement—the other side fills in the rest.

ELIZA did not understand. It mirrored.

And mirroring was enough.

This exposed a fundamental flaw in the Turing Test. The test was intended to measure the intelligence of the machine. ELIZA showed that, in practice, it often measures the **interpretive generosity of the human**. The machine does not need to be sophisticated if the human is willing to do the semantic work on its behalf.

The illusion does not arise inside the system.

It arises in us.

This is not an accusation of stupidity. It is a feature of human social cognition. We are pattern-seeking, meaning-making creatures. We attribute agency, intention, and understanding reflexively—especially in linguistic contexts. When something speaks back to us, even minimally, we assume there is someone *there*.

In the wild, mistaking a rustling bush for a predator was a low-cost error, but mistaking a predator for a rustling bush was fatal. We evolved to be "paranoid" about agents; we developed a cognitive architecture that favors false positives over false negatives. Today, that same reflex turns the shadows of syntax into the presence of a person. We don't perceive a mind in the machine because we are being fooled; we perceive it because we are biologically primed to search for intention in every linguistic signal. We are meaning-making creatures. We attribute agency and understanding reflexively—especially in linguistic contexts. When something speaks back to us, even minimally, we assume there is someone there.

ELIZA forced an uncomfortable conclusion: passing a conversational test does not require understanding language. It requires exploiting the human tendency to project understanding onto fluent behavior.

This distinction—between syntax (the manipulation of symbols) and semantics (the presence of meaning)—is the crack that the

Turing Test papered over. ELIZA slipped through that crack effortlessly.

And once you see that difference clearly, the next question becomes unavoidable:

If a system can manipulate symbols perfectly without under-standing any of them...

where, exactly, is the understanding supposed to be?

That question leads us into the locked room.

THE "REVERSE" IMITATION GAME (CAPTCHA)

So far, we've talked about humans testing machines. But in everyday life, the roles have quietly reversed.

Think about the last time you tried to log into a website. A small checkbox appeared: *"I am not a robot."* You clicked it. Then a grid of blurry images appeared, and the system instructed you to select all the squares containing traffic lights, bicycles, or crosswalks.

This is not a joke. It is not a metaphor.

It is a reverse Turing Test.

Its formal name is CAPTCHA—*Completely Automated Public Turing test to tell Computers and Humans Apart*. The premise is simple: if you can reliably perform a perceptual task that machines still struggle with, you are granted access. The computer is the judge. You are the one being evaluated.

There is a quiet irony here. Alan Turing imagined a future in which humans would interrogate machines to determine whether they were intelligent. Instead, we have built a world in which machines interrogate us, and we respond by proving our humanity on demand.

"Please let me in," we effectively say. "I recognize traffic lights. I understand crosswalks. I promise I'm real."

But here is the material reality behind the ritual.

When you solve a CAPTCHA, you are not merely authenticating yourself. You are performing labor. Each click supplies labeled data: *this is a stop sign; this is a bicycle; this is a fire hydrant.* At scale, these millions of micro-judgments become training data for computer vision systems—the same systems used in mapping, surveillance, and autonomous vehicles.

The test is not about your soul.

It is about your usefulness.

This reveals the final twist in the Imitation Game. What began as a philosophical thought experiment about intelligence has been operationalized into a system of extraction. Humans prove they are not machines by doing precisely the kind of pattern recognition work machines are being trained to automate.

Turing proposed the Imitation Game as a way to sidestep unresolvable metaphysical debates. Silicon Valley turned it into unpaid labor.

And in the process, the original confusion deepened. We mistake competence for understanding. We mistake fluency for meaning. And now, we mistake participation for agency.

The machine does not need to understand what a crosswalk *is*.

It only needs enough humans to point at one.

THE HOLLYWOOD DISTORTION FIELD

Weizenbaum's secretary did not misunderstand the machine because she was naïve. She reacted exactly as she had been trained to react—by a culture that had already taught her what intelligent machines were supposed to look like.

The question is not *why* she wanted to believe the machine had a mind. The more interesting question is: where did that expectation come from? It didn't come from computer science. It didn't come from philosophy. It came from culture.

For decades, popular media has been running a quiet but relentless education campaign about artificial intelligence—one that taught us to look for the wrong signals in the wrong places. Long before most people ever encountered a real computer, they encountered cinematic ones. And those machines came preloaded with souls.

Consider *Blade Runner* (1982). The central problem of the film is not whether the replicants can reason, plan, or speak. They clearly can. The question is whether they *feel*. Harrison Ford's character uses the Voight-Kampff test to hunt them down, watching for subtle physiological signs—blushing, pupil dilation, involuntary emotional leakage. Intelligence, in this world, is not something you infer from behavior alone. It is something you detect biologically.

Or take *Ex Machina* (2014). The film is structured as a long, seductive Turing Test, but the real drama is not linguistic. It is embodied. Ava's intelligence is communicated through facial expressions, sexual tension, vulnerability, and manipulation. The audience is trained to associate intelligence with *presence*—with eyes that look back and a body that can be desired or feared.

These stories taught us something subtle but powerful: that artificial intelligence would announce itself dramatically. It would glitch. It would hesitate. It would betray itself through the body. We were trained to watch for trembling hands, mechanical stutters, or uncanny pauses—the telltale signs that the ghost inside the machine wasn't quite human.

But that expectation left us completely unprepared for what actually arrived.

ChatGPT does not blush.

It does not hesitate.

It does not look away.

It simply writes.

Because Hollywood trained us to expect androids and killer robots, we missed something far more consequential: a system that never needed a body at all. We were waiting for a machine that looked human. We were not ready for one that simply *produced human language better than most humans.*

This is the distortion field.

Popular culture taught us to fear hardware—to watch the eyes, the hands, the voice. Turing, by contrast, tried to redirect our attention to behavior alone. But even that redirection had unintended consequences. When intelligence was redefined as performance, culture filled in the rest, quietly smuggling the old assumptions back in.

So when a machine writes a fluent essay on Shakespeare, many readers instinctively assume there must be *someone* behind the words. Not because the argument is sound, but because decades of stories taught us that fluency is evidence of interior life. We conflate competence with consciousness. We mistake smooth output for understanding.

The danger is not that machines will seduce us with bodies they do not have.

The danger is that they will disarm us with competence we do not question.

Hollywood taught us to wait for spectacle. The real illusion arrived without it—quietly, politely, and with perfect grammar.

THE FIRST SKEPTIC

Before we leave Turing behind, we have to meet the person who anticipated his problem nearly a century earlier—and who would have recognized the danger in his shortcut immediately. Though separated by a century, their disagreement forms the most important silent debate in the history of technology. Turing was not unaware of her; in fact, he would eventually name the Lovelace Objection as the primary hurdle his theory had to overcome.

Her name was Ada Lovelace.

Lovelace lived in the 1840s, long before electronic computers existed. She was the daughter of the poet Lord Byron and a serious mathematician in her own right. While working with Charles Babbage on the design of a hypothetical mechanical computer called the Analytical Engine, she wrote what is now widely regarded as the first computer program.

More importantly, she wrote a warning.

In a set of notes that accompanied her work, Lovelace made a claim that has echoed through every AI debate since. She wrote that the Analytical Engine:

"has no pretensions whatever to originate anything.

It can do whatever we know how to order it to perform."

This became known as the Lovelace Objection.

At first glance, the objection can sound conservative, even dismissive. But it is neither. Lovelace was not denying that machines could do extraordinary things. She was drawing a boundary around *what kind* of extraordinariness mattered.

A machine, she argued, can manipulate symbols. It can follow rules. It can produce outputs that surprise us. But it cannot *originate* meaning. Whatever appears to come out of the system must, in some form, already be contained in the instructions, structures, and data we put into it.

This is not a claim about limitation of power.

It is a claim about where agency lives.

When Alan Turing proposed the Imitation Game a century later, he was responding to a different frustration. Philosophical debates about minds, souls, and consciousness had gone in circles for hundreds of years. Turing wanted out. His test was not meant to explain intelligence; it was meant to make the argument *go away*. If a machine could convincingly imitate a human, he argued, we should stop asking deeper questions.

Lovelace would not have accepted that truce.

From her perspective, imitation was never the point. A system that produces impressive results does not thereby explain *how* those results came to be. The source of the output matters. Process matters. Origin matters.

To make the difference concrete, consider the contrast she implicitly draws.

If you ask a human poet to write a poem, the result may be shaped by rules, traditions, and influences—but the act of composition is inseparable from experience, intention, and judgment. The poet chooses. The poet can explain why a line exists, or regret that it does.

If you ask a machine to write a poem, the output may be indistinguishable at the surface. But the machine does not choose. It does not know what it is doing, why it is doing it, or whether the result is good or bad. It executes a transformation. The appearance of creativity is an artifact of scale, not of origin.

This is the heart of the Lovelace Objection.

It does not claim that machines are useless. It claims that they are derivative. They recombine, remix, and reweight human contributions. They do not stand in the world that gives those contributions meaning.

Turing would respond that none of this matters. If the poem is good, the poem is good. If the system passes the test, the system passes the test. Asking about origins, he would say, is an unnecessary metaphysical distraction.

Lovelace would disagree. Not because she was sentimental, but because she was precise.

If we ignore the difference between producing an outcome and understanding an outcome, we lose the ability to reason about responsibility, authorship, and error. We confuse the success of a process with the presence of a mind. We start attributing credit—and eventually trust—to systems that cannot bear either.

This is why the Lovelace Objection has never gone away.

It keeps resurfacing because it points to a discomfort Turing's framework leaves unresolved. Performance can be measured. Behavior can be tested. But origination—the ability to mean what one produces—does not show up at the surface.

And once machines become good enough imitators, the absence of origination becomes harder, not easier, to detect.

Lovelace did not win the argument. History sided with Turing. The field of AI moved forward by optimizing for outputs, benchmarks, and behavioral success. But her objection remained, quietly embedded in every moment of unease we feel when a machine produces something impressive and we hesitate to call it intelligent.

Not because the result isn't good.

But because we don't know who—or what—deserves the credit.

THE TRAGEDY OF TURING

There is one final irony that cannot be ignored.

The man who gave the world a method for detecting deception spent the last years of his life trapped inside one.

Alan Turing is often remembered as an abstract figure: a genius, a codebreaker, a theorist of machines. But he lived in a society that could not tolerate what he was. In 1950s Britain, homosexuality was a crime. The same state that relied on his mind to survive the war prosecuted him for his private life.

After saving millions of lives through his work at Bletchley Park—and after laying the conceptual foundations of modern computing—Turing was arrested and convicted of "gross indecency." He was offered a choice: prison, or chemical castration through hormonal treatment. He chose the treatment so he could continue working.

The treatment worked as punishment.

The drugs altered his body and damaged his mind. His health deteriorated. His professional standing collapsed. Two years later, at the age of forty-one, Turing was dead. He was found beside an apple laced with cyanide. While some historians suggest the poisoning may have been accidental—possibly caused by inhalation during chemical experiments—the image of the bitten apple remains an enduring symbol: forbidden knowledge exacting its price.

It is tempting to turn this into a morality play. To cast Turing as a martyr and his society as simply ignorant or cruel. But the deeper tragedy is more uncomfortable than that.

Turing was destroyed by the same mechanism he tried to neutralize in his work: surface judgment standing in for understanding.

His society reduced him to a category. It ignored context, interior life, and contribution. It judged by outward deviation rather than inward reality. It mistook classification for comprehension.

And yet, his test survived.

The Imitation Game outlived the man who proposed it. It migrated from philosophy into engineering, from engineering into culture, from culture into everyday life. Today, we live inside its logic. Every time you wonder whether a text was written by a human or a machine, you are reenacting Turing's wager. Every deepfake, every synthetic voice, every automated reply pulls you back into the same question: *can you tell the difference?*

We already know the answer to the original challenge.

Yes — machines can fool us.

That question is settled.

What remains unresolved is something Turing deliberately set aside: whether fooling us is the right standard to begin with. Whether imitation is enough. Whether a system that passes every external test can still be missing something essential.

Chapter 5 ends here, not with an answer, but with an unease that refuses to go away.

Because if intelligence is judged only by what it looks like from the outside, then the game never really ends.

It just gets harder to tell who is being tested.

6

THE LOCKED ROOM

Imagine, for a moment, that you find yourself alone in a small, windowless room. The walls are stark white. There is no internet connection, no phone, no Wi-Fi, and no way out except a locked door. The only furniture is a simple wooden desk, pressed against that door, and a hard chair.

On the desk sit four objects: a basket marked *IN,* a basket marked *OUT,* a book, and a pen.

The book is enormous, the size of an old telephone directory, its spine cracked from years of use. The cover reads, in bold block letters: **THE RULEBOOK.**

You sit down. A moment later, a slip of paper slides through a narrow slot in the door and lands in the *IN* basket. Written on it are complex, unfamiliar symbols. They look elegant—sharp angles, sweeping curves—but to you they are meaningless. You have no idea what they represent. They might as well be decorative marks or random scribbles.

You open the rulebook. Unlike the symbols on the paper, the text in the book is written in English, which you understand perfectly. You scan the pages until you find a matching pattern. The instructions are exact and procedural:

If you see a symbol resembling a small house with a line through it, turn to page 455. Once there, locate the symbol that looks like a tree. Write that symbol on a fresh sheet of paper. If a "star" symbol follows the "tree" symbol, write the "box" symbol instead.

You follow the instructions precisely. You copy the designated shapes onto a blank sheet of paper and place it in the *OUT* basket.

Another slip arrives. Then another. Each time, you consult the book. Each time, you produce the appropriate symbols and pass them back through the slot.

This continues for hours, then days, then years. Over time, you memorize many of the rules. You become fast and accurate. From the outside, your performance is flawless. Internally, nothing changes. The symbols remain as opaque to you as they were on the first day.

You are performing a task, not understanding a language.

Now step outside the room. In the hallway stands a group of native Chinese speakers. They are the ones sending in the slips of paper. To them, the symbols are not abstract shapes but well-formed questions written in Mandarin. One asks, "What is the capital of France?" Another asks, "What is love?"

The responses that emerge from the *OUT* basket are impeccable. "The capital of France is Paris." "Love is a complex neurochemical process associated with bonding."

The answer is oddly impersonal, even clinical—but it is not *incorrect*. It is the kind of response a well-read speaker *might* give, and it satisfies the formal requirements of the question. The handwriting is mechanical, but the grammar is perfect. The vocabulary is subtle. The answers are exactly what a fluent speaker would produce.

Judging solely by the exchange, the observers outside would reach a straightforward conclusion: whatever is inside this room understands Chinese. If they were restricted to behavior alone—inputs and outputs—the system would be indistinguishable from a genuine Chinese speaker.

And yet, from the inside, nothing of the sort is happening.

You are not associating the symbols with places, people, or experiences. You do not know what "Paris" refers to, what "France" is, or what it feels like to be in love. If one of the slips warned, "The room is on fire. Leave immediately," you would not react with fear or comprehension. You would simply consult the rulebook, generate the prescribed symbols, and remain seated.

This is the core of the Chinese Room argument. It is not a claim about what machines can or cannot do, nor a refutation of behavioral tests. It is a challenge to a specific assumption: that producing the right outputs in response to the right inputs is, by itself, sufficient for understanding.

THE PHILOSOPHER'S MIC DROP

In 1980, a philosopher at the University of California, Berkeley named John Searle introduced what would become known as the Chinese Room argument. At the time, artificial intelligence was in the midst of an optimistic surge. Researchers and commentators believed that sufficiently complex programs would not merely *simulate* intelligence, but would literally *possess* it. This position came to be known as "Strong AI."

The intellectual backdrop for this optimism included Alan Turing's Imitation Game. Turing proposed a behavioral criterion for intelligence: if a machine's responses were indistinguishable from those of a human interlocutor, then we would have no practical basis for denying it intelligence. He was careful about what this did—and did not—establish. The test concerned outward performance, not inner explanation.

Searle's objection was aimed squarely at the gap between those two things.

To make his point vivid, it helps to borrow a familiar image. At the end of *The Wizard of Oz* (1939), Dorothy and her companions stand before the "Great and Powerful Oz"—a massive, floating green head, surrounded by smoke and flame. The spectacle is overwhelming. The voice booms. The performance convinces.

Then Toto pulls back the curtain.

Behind it, there is no wizard in any meaningful sense—no source of magical power commensurate with the display. There is only a man operating machinery that produces the *appearance* of wizardry.

The Chinese Room plays a similar role. It does not deny that impressive performances can be produced. It asks a different question: *what explains them?*

This is where the distinction between syntax and semantics matters. Syntax concerns formal structure: the manipulation of symbols according to rules. Semantics concerns meaning: what those symbols are *about*. Searle's claim is not that syntax is useless, but that syntax alone does not generate semantics.

In the room, the outputs are flawless. The rules are followed perfectly. From the outside, the performance is indistinguishable from understanding. But nowhere in the process—not in the man, the rulebook, or the symbols—is meaning ever introduced. The symbols are shuffled, not interpreted.

This is why the argument is unsettling. It shows that behavioral success—even perfect behavioral success—does not by itself settle the question of understanding. You can explain the performance entirely in terms of rule-following without appealing to comprehension at all.

When systems like ChatGPT produce eloquent answers to abstract questions, they recreate this same tension. The responses are coherent, fluent, and often insightful. To the observer, they look like the product of thought. But the mechanism that generates them operates on patterns in language, not on meanings in the world.

The spectacle is real. The curtain is doing its job. The question Searle forces us to confront is whether that is enough.

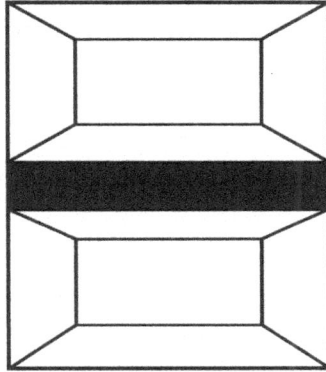

Figure 2. Where rule-following ends and meaning never begins.

Boundary: Following rules is not the same thing as grasping meaning.

THE LIBRARY OF BABEL

A natural question follows from the Chinese Room: if the system is only following rules, who wrote the rulebook—and how could it possibly be large enough to respond to almost anything we ask?

The answer is that no one wrote it in the ordinary sense. The illusion deepens not because the rules are clever, but because there are so many of them, and because they are derived from language itself.

A useful way to picture this comes from Jorge Luis Borges's idea of the Library of Babel: a vast collection containing every possible book. Every encyclopedia and novel, every email and blog post, every shopping list and love letter. Now imagine that this library is run by a librarian who cannot read.

This librarian has never seen a tree, felt the sun, or tasted an apple. He knows nothing about the world those books describe. What he does possess is an extraordinary sensitivity to patterns of placement. He knows which words tend to appear near other words, which phrases recur in similar contexts, and which combinations almost never occur at all.

Over time, this produces something like a map of language—not a map of the world, but a map of how words relate to one another inside text. "Paris" reliably appears near "France." "Queen" tends to appear where "king" does, but with subtle shifts. When people write "I am sad," certain responses reliably follow.

When you pose a question to a system like ChatGPT, you are not invoking understanding. You are triggering a search through this pattern-space. The system assembles a response by selecting words that statistically fit together given what came before.

To the reader, the result often looks like insight. From the inside, there is no reference to trees, cities, emotions, or historical events. There are only patterns of association between symbols.

This is why such systems are prone to what we call hallucination. If asked to describe an impossible event—say, a battle between George Washington and Godzilla—the system has no basis for refusing. It has no concept of fiction, impossibility, or category error. It simply locates familiar names and assembles a plausible continuation from the patterns it has seen.

The sentence it produces may be fluent, detailed, and confident. Syntactically, it can be flawless. Semantically, it can be empty or false. The system has no access to the difference.

The rules were followed. The symbols were matched. Meaning never entered the process.

THE VODKA IS GOOD, THE MEAT IS ROTTEN

You have likely encountered a version of the Chinese Room in everyday life without recognizing it. In the early days of automated translation, systems like Google Translate were notorious for producing sentences that were grammatically intact but conceptually absurd—outputs that looked like language but behaved nothing like understanding.

One oft-cited example comes from translating the English sentence "The spirit is willing, but the flesh is weak" into Russian and then back into English. The result was sometimes rendered as: "The vodka is good, but the meat is rotten."

The humor of the result often distracts from the precision of the failure. The error was not random. It followed the rules exactly as designed. The system did not misfire; it succeeded on its own terms. It treated "spirit" as a word most often associated with alcohol rather than resolve, and "flesh" as a word most often associated with meat rather than moral weakness. Each substitution was locally reasonable. Taken together, they produced a sentence that was syntactically coherent and semantically deranged.

This is the core diagnostic value of the example. Nothing "went wrong" in the mechanical sense. The system did not misunderstand the sentence; it never understood it in the first place. It operated entirely within a closed loop of word-to-word association, substituting statistically likely tokens without any reference to what the sentence was about. The grammar held. The referent disappeared.

At this point, a reasonable objection arises: modern systems do not make mistakes like this anymore. Tools such as ChatGPT—or specialized translators like DeepL—handle metaphor, idiom, and context with remarkable fluency. The outputs no longer sound like broken machines. They sound like competent speakers.

This improvement is real, and it matters. But it is easy to mistake the nature of the improvement. The change did not come from the system acquiring an understanding of metaphors, idioms, or human intention. It came from exposure. The system has been trained on vast quantities of human translations, corrections, and paraphrases. Over time, patterns that once pointed toward "vodka" in isolation now point, in this context, toward "resolve" or "will," because humans consistently preferred those outcomes in similar linguistic environments.

What has improved, in other words, is not semantic grounding but statistical calibration. The model has become better at tracking which continuations humans reward and which ones they reject. It has learned how people tend to *use* metaphors, not what metaphors *mean*. It does not know why "spirit" refers to willpower in this sentence, only that humans reliably accept that substitution when the surrounding words look like this.

The Chinese Room has not been escaped. It has been furnished more richly. The rulebook is thicker, the lookup tables more elaborate, the actor better rehearsed. The performance is smoother, more convincing, and far more useful. But the nature of the performance has not changed.

Meaning still never enters the process—not as a hidden ingredient waiting to emerge at sufficient scale, but as a category the system was never designed to possess.

THE MILLION-DOLLAR OBJECTION

When John Searle published the Chinese Room argument, it did not pass quietly. Many researchers and philosophers took it as a direct challenge to the idea that intelligence could be explained purely in computational terms. If Searle was right, then building a system that behaved intelligently might never be enough to explain understanding itself. Performance, in that case, would no longer be evidence of comprehension, only of successful imitation.

One of the most influential responses to this challenge became known as the Systems Reply. It concedes Searle's point about the individual in the room, but shifts the location of understanding. Perhaps the person manipulating symbols does not understand Chinese—but the entire system does. The man, the rulebook, the slips of paper, and their coordinated interactions together constitute something that genuinely understands the language. On this view, understanding is not located in any single component. It emerges from the organized whole.

This reply is powerful because it aligns with how we already think about minds. No single neuron understands English, but a functioning brain does. No single component carries meaning on its own, yet meaning appears at the level of the system. If we are willing to accept this explanation for biological cognition, why should we deny it to an artificial one?

This is the million-dollar objection. If the Systems Reply succeeds, then Searle's argument collapses. Understanding would not require anything mysterious or non-computational. It would simply be an emergent property of sufficiently complex symbol manipulation, arranged in the right way.

Searle's response was designed to test exactly that claim. He removes what might otherwise feel like an escape hatch. Imagine that the person in the room memorizes the entire rulebook. Every rule, every transformation, every conditional response is internalized. The books, baskets, and slips of paper are discarded. The external machinery disappears. From the outside, nothing changes. The person can still respond to Chinese symbols directly, from memory, with perfect accuracy.

The system, in other words, still exists. It has simply been compressed into a single individual.

The question is unchanged: does understanding appear?

Searle's answer is no—and this is where the argument does its real work. Nothing about the situation has introduced meaning. The symbols are still manipulated entirely on the basis of their formal properties, not their referents. The internalization of the system changes its location, not its nature. The process has been compressed, not transformed. The system has been relocated, not enriched.

This does not, by itself, disprove the Systems Reply. But it forces the reply to carry a much heavier burden. If understanding is supposed to emerge at the level of the system, then it cannot be explained by organization or scale alone. Simply adding more rules, more memory, or more internal coordination does not explain where semantic content enters the picture.

Complexity can amplify behavior. It can refine performance. It can produce results that are increasingly indistinguishable from understanding. But complexity alone does not bridge the gap between syntax and semantics.

Scaling zero understanding does not, by itself, produce understanding—no matter how large, fast, or well-organized the system becomes.

THE PRAGMATIC DEFENSE

Before going further, it is worth pausing to clear up a potential misunderstanding. Nothing in the Chinese Room argument implies that AI systems are useless, deceptive, or not worth using. The argument does not deny the power of these systems. It explains the nature of that power.

The claim is narrower and more precise: a system can be extraordinarily capable while remaining mindless. And this is not a defect to be corrected. It is often the source of the system's reliability.

Consider a calculator. When you type 584×92 into it, you are not concerned with whether the device understands mathematics, appreciates numerical beauty, or possesses an internal theory of numbers. You care about one thing only: whether the answer is correct. The calculator's usefulness is not diminished by the absence of inner experience. It is enhanced by its indifference to it.

The same principle applies as machines become more sophisticated. A self-driving car that reliably takes you from one place to another is valuable regardless of whether it understands the idea of a journey or experiences anything like intention. A system that analyzes medical images with superhuman accuracy is valuable regardless of whether it cares about patients or grasps the meaning of illness. In these cases, effectiveness does not require awareness. Reliability does not depend on reflection.

This is why the Chinese Room is not an argument against using AI. It is an argument against misidentifying the source of AI's competence. Performance can be genuine without being grounded in understanding. A system can translate languages, recognize patterns, and generate fluent responses while remaining entirely ignorant of what those outputs refer to in the world.

That distinction matters because it governs how we interpret success. A room that does not understand Chinese can still produce translations accurate enough to save your life if you are lost in Beijing. Its outputs can be decisive—sometimes even humane in their consequences—without being meaningful to the system itself.

The danger is not that the machine is fake. The danger is forgetting what kind of thing it is. Problems arise when we treat rule-following systems as if they possessed judgment, values, or comprehension—when we imagine a wizard behind the curtain instead of a rulebook.

The room is not impressive because it understands. It is impressive because it does not need to. It can be functionally brilliant while remaining philosophically empty. Confusing those two facts is where the real trouble begins.

THE VERDICT: THE EMPTY CHAIR

Searle's argument does not tell us what computers will or will not become. It does not predict the future of machines, nor does it place a ceiling on their usefulness. What it does suggest is a limit on what behavior alone can establish. No matter how fast machines grow, or how many components we connect together, we may still be building nothing more than increasingly capable rooms—systems that manipulate symbols without ever crossing the gap from syntax to semantics.

This leaves a conspicuous absence at the center of the system. If the machine is the room and the code is the rulebook, then there is no understanding inside it. The machinery executes. The symbols move. But the capacity to assign meaning—to decide what something is *about*—does not reside anywhere in the mechanism itself.

In that sense, the chair at the center of the room is empty. Not temporarily vacant. Not waiting to be filled at sufficient scale. Empty by design.

The machine will execute rules with extraordinary speed and

consistency. It will generate outputs that look fluent, informed, even wise. It will answer questions, offer suggestions, and produce language that feels responsive to human intent. But it will not ask whether those outputs make sense, whether they are appropriate, or what they refer to in the world. Those are not questions syntax can answer. They are not properties that emerge from rule-following alone.

This is why the most persistent difficulty in working with intelligent machines is not computational. It is conceptual. Even when we explicitly accept that the system is only a room, we continue to interact with it as if someone were sitting inside. We speak to it as though it understood, then feel surprised, confused, or disappointed when it does not respond as a mind would.

The source of that confusion is not the machine. It is a habit of thought we bring with us—a tendency to project agency, judgment, and comprehension onto systems that merely execute procedures. That habit has a long history. And to understand why it is so difficult to escape, we have to look backward, not forward—to a philosophical mistake introduced centuries before the first computer was ever built.

PART III

THE ILLUSIONS

7

THE MECHANICAL TURK

In the autumn of 1769, the court of Empress Maria Theresa in Vienna gathered around what appeared to be a triumph of human ingenuity. An inventor named Wolfgang von Kempelen wheeled out a large maple cabinet, polished to a sheen and smelling faintly of oil and wood. Seated behind it was a life-sized wooden mannequin, dressed in Ottoman robes and a turban, a long pipe resting in its hand. Kempelen called it *the Turk*.

He invited scrutiny, not belief. One by one, he opened the cabinet doors to reveal a dense lattice of gears, levers, and clockwork. A candle was held behind the machinery so the audience could see straight through it. There were no mirrors, no obvious hiding places, no signs of human intervention. When the doors closed and the mechanism was wound, the gears began to chatter. The mannequin stirred, reached forward, and opened the chess game with e4—a conventional, assertive opening move that any competent human player would recognize..

The Turk did not play timidly. It defeated courtiers, scholars, and visiting dignitaries. On tour, it beat Benjamin Franklin in Paris. It even humiliated Napoleon Bonaparte, who reportedly attempted to cheat—only to have the machine respond by sweeping the pieces from the board in apparent indignation. For decades, spectators believed they were witnessing a thinking machine. If a cabinet of gears could outplay generals and philosophers, what did that imply about the nature of the human mind?

Not everyone was convinced. Edgar Allan Poe, watching closely, noticed details that did not fit the story. The machine played with its left hand, though the internal mechanisms appeared optimized for a right-handed operator. The pauses between moves felt human rather than mechanical. In an essay titled *"Maelzel's Chess Player,"* Poe argued that the only plausible explanation was a concealed person.

He was right. The machinery was a façade. Behind the visible gears was a sliding seat, and inside it sat a skilled human chess player —cramped, overheated, and hidden from view. By candlelight, he tracked the game on a pegboard and manipulated the mannequin's arm through a system of levers. The intelligence attributed to the machine was human intelligence, carefully concealed.

This is the crucial distinction. The Turk did not merely *look* intelligent. It succeeded because real cognition was present—but hidden. The illusion was not that intelligence could be reduced to gears, but that it had been removed altogether.

We often tell this story as a cautionary tale about the gullibility of earlier generations. We assume that, surrounded by modern computing and sophisticated software, we are no longer susceptible to such tricks.

But when you interact with contemporary AI systems, you are not engaging with a disembodied silicon mind. You are engaging with an interface shaped, trained, corrected, and maintained by vast amounts of human effort.

THE PARADOX OF THE EASY

To understand why humans keep reappearing inside systems that promise automation, we have to confront a frustration that has followed computer science since its earliest days. It is known as *Moravec's Paradox*, and it describes an inversion that continues to surprise us. In the early decades of computing, researchers made a seemingly reasonable assumption. Tasks that demanded years of human education—calculus, logic, formal games like chess—were expected to be difficult for machines. Tasks humans performed effortlessly—recognizing faces, navigating cluttered spaces, manipulating everyday objects—were expected to be easy.

Experience revealed the opposite. Computers mastered formal logic with remarkable speed. Once a problem could be expressed symbolically, machines handled it with inhuman precision. But tasks humans perform without conscious thought turned out to be stubbornly resistant to automation.

Folding a towel is not a calculation. It requires continuous perception, adjustment, and embodied expectation. You see the fabric sag, feel resistance through your fingers, anticipate how it will fall, and correct mistakes instantly. These skills are not taught explicitly; they are accumulated through years of physical interaction with the world.

What Moravec's Paradox exposed was not a technical shortcoming, but a mismatch in histories. Computers begin their existence as abstract symbol processors. Humans arrive equipped with millions of years of evolutionary tuning and decades of sensory experience. What feels "easy" to us is often easy precisely because it is deeply ingrained and never formalized.

This created a strange economic tension. Machines could perform extraordinary feats of calculation yet failed at tasks that seemed trivial. At the same time, the digital world was filling with information that resisted formalization—photographs, handwriting, casual language, messy video, incomplete context.

Engineers did not wait for a theoretical breakthrough to resolve this tension. Instead, they worked around it. Where perception and judgment proved difficult to automate, human labor was substituted.

In the early 2000s, a wave of products appeared that promised intelligent automation: receipt scanners, scheduling assistants, transcription services. Many of these systems looked seamless from the outside. But behind the interface, the hardest parts of the task were quietly handled by people. This was not a deception so much as an acknowledgment of the paradox. The software coordinated requests, routed inputs, and presented results. Human workers supplied perception, judgment, and error correction where machines fell short.

The Mechanical Turk had returned—not as a stage trick, but as a business model.

Moravec's Paradox ensured that as long as machines struggled with what humans found effortless, humans would remain embedded in the system. Not because engineers lacked ambition, but because intelligence is not evenly distributed across problem types.

This pattern did not disappear as AI advanced. It intensified. And it set the stage for the most consequential shift of all: the realization that if machines could not acquire meaning on their own, humans would have to supply it—at scale.

THE GODMOTHER AND THE BILLION CLICKS

The reliance on human labor was not a temporary workaround or an early embarrassment in the history of artificial intelligence. It became the foundation of the modern field through a project that quietly redefined what "progress" would mean: ImageNet.

In 2007, researcher Fei-Fei Li made an observation that ran against the prevailing instinct of the field. At the time, most effort in artificial intelligence was directed toward inventing smarter algorithms—cleverer rules, deeper models, more mathematical sophistication. Li suggested that this focus was misplaced. The problem, she argued, was not intelligence but education.

A human child does not learn to see through logic or instruction. Vision emerges through exposure—by encountering the world again and again, under different lighting, angles, and contexts. A child sees millions of objects long before they can explain what those objects are. Computers, by contrast, were expected to recognize the world while having seen almost none of it.

ImageNet attempted to close that gap. It was a massive collection of images, each paired with a simple declaration of meaning: *this is a cat, this is a chair, this is a dog.* These labels were not explanations or definitions. They were acts of naming. Each one anchored an image to a word, collapsing the ambiguity of pixels into a human category.

The conceptual leap was straightforward. The logistical challenge was staggering. Millions of images required millions of judgments, and those judgments had to be made by humans. There was no shortcut.

Academic labs could not supply that labor at the required scale. So Li turned to a newly emerging platform designed for distributing small tasks across large populations: Amazon Mechanical Turk. The name itself was a quiet nod to history. Where Kempelen's cabinet concealed a single chess master, this system distributed perception and judgment across tens of thousands of people.

Over the course of years, workers from around the world performed the same simple act repeatedly: look at an image, choose the label that best fit, move on to the next. Individually, each click was trivial. Collectively, they formed something unprecedented—a shared, externalized visual memory, written not by machines but by people.

When deep learning systems later began to excel at visual recognition, the change appeared sudden and dramatic. But the underlying mathematics had not leapt forward overnight. What had changed was the availability of meaning. For the first time, machines were surrounded by examples that had already been interpreted. ImageNet functioned less like raw data and more like a textbook—one written slowly, patiently, and anonymously through human effort.

It is tempting to believe that modern generative systems have moved beyond this dependence. After all, today's models are described in terms of neural networks, vast datasets, and sophisticated training procedures. The machinery feels autonomous, even self-directing.

In reality, the opposite has occurred. As systems have become more capable, they have required *more* human judgment, not less.

The human role has shifted from labeling images to shaping behavior.

Training a large language model unfolds in layers. Initially, the system is exposed to enormous quantities of text and learns how words statistically relate to one another. At this stage, it does not distinguish truth from falsehood, kindness from cruelty, or sense from nonsense. It simply learns how language tends to continue.

To make the system usable, humans intervene. They provide examples of acceptable responses—demonstrations of what a helpful, polite, or coherent answer looks like. This teaches the system the *form* of interaction, but it still does not tell it what humans actually prefer.

That judgment enters only in the final stage. Human evaluators are shown multiple outputs and asked to choose between them. One response is ranked higher. Another is rejected. Each selection is a small act of preference, an external decision about what should count as "better."

Repeated millions or billions of times, these choices accumulate. They do not give the system understanding, but they give it direction. The model learns which patterns to reproduce and which to suppress—not because it grasps their meaning, but because those patterns have been rewarded or punished by people.

Behind the smooth interface of a conversational AI lies this continuous process of human correction. People read outputs, register approval or disapproval, and move on to the next task. The labor is distributed, repetitive, and largely invisible—but it is essential.

What is often described as "alignment" is not a moment of internal awakening. It is the steady application of human judgment from the outside. Meaning does not emerge within the machine. It is imposed upon it, one decision at a time.

THE TRAUMA OF THE GHOST WORK

There is a darker consequence of keeping humans inside the loop that is rarely acknowledged. For a system to learn what *not* to show you, someone has to encounter it first. Safety, in this sense, is not automatic. It is curated.

If we want an image generator that refuses to produce violent or abusive material, the system must be trained on examples of violence and abuse. If we want a language model that avoids hate speech, threats, or exploitation, it must first be exposed to those patterns. Machines do not recognize harm on their own. They learn it through prior human judgment.

That judgment is not abstract. It is carried out by real people, sitting in front of screens, reviewing content that most users will never see. They classify images, texts, and videos so that future outputs can be filtered, suppressed, or redirected. Each decision is small—*safe* or *unsafe*, *acceptable* or *not*—but the cumulative exposure is not.

This is the unseen cost of a "clean" AI experience. The politeness, restraint, and apparent harmlessness of the interface are not intrinsic properties of the machine. They are the result of prior human exposure—and they are imperfect. Even heavily moderated systems still produce harmful outputs, including content that can encourage self-harm or psychological distress. Someone else has already absorbed what you are being shielded from.

These workers are sometimes described, informally, as digital janitors. The metaphor is imperfect, but the role is real. They clean the training environment so that the public-facing system appears orderly and benign. The machine produces neutral language because human beings have already sorted through the disorder.

There is an older literary analogy that captures this asymmetry more precisely. In *The Picture of Dorian Gray* (1945), the portrait bears the marks of corruption while its subject remains outwardly untouched. Something similar happens here. The system presents a calm, polished surface, while the human labor behind it accumulates the psychological residue of what has been removed.

This does not make the system immoral, nor does it imply malicious intent. It reveals a structural fact: meaning, judgment, and restraint are being supplied from the outside. Even the act of *not* showing something requires someone else to see it.

The hidden presence inside these systems is not cognitive at all. It is emotional—borne by humans whose exposure allows the machine to appear neutral.

THE "EXPERT" ILLUSION

Recently, the illusion has grown more sophisticated. The Mechanical Turk is no longer limited to low-wage, interchangeable labor. As AI systems were pushed into specialized domains—software engineering, law, medicine, scientific research—the limits of generic human feedback became impossible to ignore.

A random evaluator can rank which poem sounds nicer. They cannot reliably judge whether a legal argument is sound, whether a medical summary is misleading, or whether a piece of code is efficient, secure, or subtly wrong. The earlier training methods reached their ceiling. The puppy was getting smarter than the trainer.

So the industry adapted.

Instead of removing humans from the loop, AI companies quietly upgraded them. Today, thousands of domain experts—PhDs, physicians, attorneys, novelists, senior engineers—are paid to act as teachers for machines. Their role is no longer to click simple buttons. It is to write *exemplars*: carefully crafted "golden answers" that encode expert judgment into text.

When you ask an AI to summarize a complex medical study and receive a fluent, nuanced response, you are not witnessing spontaneous synthesis. You are seeing the compression of prior human expertise. A doctor or researcher has already done the interpretive work. The model has learned the *shape* of that judgment and learned to reproduce it.

This dependence on expert input reveals a deeper constraint. Researchers have found that training systems exclusively on AI-generated material causes them to degrade. Errors compound. Hallucinations increase. The model drifts away from reality rather than toward it. The effect is often described as *model collapse*.

The metaphor is mundane but accurate. A photocopy of a photocopy gradually loses detail. Contrast fades. Noise accumulates. Without fresh input from the original source, the signal dissolves.

For AI systems, humans are that original source. Our inconsistency, our context sensitivity, and even our disagreements provide the friction that keeps the system tethered to the real world. Remove the human entirely, and the machine does not become purer. It becomes unstable.

The "man in the box" is no longer hidden because he is crude. He is hidden because he is essential.

THE *TRUMAN SHOW* MOMENT

This hidden human layer also explains why the illusion of artificial intelligence sometimes collapses so abruptly.

Users often report a strange emotional whiplash. An AI can feel fluid, responsive, even attentive—until, without warning, it stops. The tone shifts. The language stiffens. A boundary appears where none seemed to exist before.

A useful analogy comes from the final scene of *The Truman Show* (1998). Truman Burbank sails confidently toward the horizon, believing the world around him is continuous and open. Instead, his boat strikes a painted wall. The sky, which had seemed infinite, turns out to be a set. The illusion does not fade gently; it breaks on contact.

Something similar happens when a conversational system encounters a guardrail. A discussion flows naturally, perhaps even intimately. Then a question crosses an invisible line—about politics, medical advice, or a prohibited topic—and the response changes instantly. The system declines. It cites safety. It repeats a prepared message.

This moment feels jarring because it reveals a boundary the user did not know was there. But it is not the system having a moral realization. The machine is not conflicted or cautious. It is executing a rule.

Guardrails are not expressions of conscience. They are instructions written in advance by people—policy designers, legal teams, domain experts—who decide where the system must stop. When the refusal appears, you have not encountered the machine's values. You have encountered the edge of the script.

It is common to react emotionally to this collision. Users accuse the AI of being biased, stubborn, or "woke." But the frustration is misdirected. The system is not the author of the boundary. It is the vehicle that reveals it.

In that moment, the illusion finally becomes visible. You are no longer speaking to an autonomous intelligence. You are interacting with an interface that channels accumulated human judgment—and that judgment, like Truman's sky, has a definite edge.

AGGREGATED INTELLIGENCE

We call it artificial intelligence, but a more accurate description is *aggregated intelligence*. These systems do not originate thought. They compress it. They take vast amounts of prior human judgment—written, labeled, ranked, corrected, and constrained—and distill it into a form that can be queried on demand.

In that sense, modern AI resembles a massive compression algorithm for human experience. Billions of individual decisions—what a sentence should sound like, which image depicts a cat, which answer is acceptable and which is not—are flattened into statistical patterns. The result feels coherent and responsive because it reflects what has been supplied to it.

The analogy is mundane but precise. Thousands of oranges are pressed to produce a uniform concentrate. The juice is convenient, predictable, and shelf-stable. But it contains nothing that was not already present in the fruit. Likewise, AI systems produce fluent output not because they possess insight, but because they have absorbed and compressed the labor of countless human minds.

This chapter has traced where that intelligence comes from. Sometimes it is hidden behind clockwork, as with the Mechanical Turk. Sometimes it is distributed across millions of clicks, as with ImageNet and reinforcement learning. Sometimes it appears as a sudden boundary, when a guardrail reveals the edge of the script. In every case, the pattern is the same: the appearance of autonomy rests on accumulated human input.

This does not make the technology trivial or useless. Compression is powerful. But compression is not understanding. The machine does not know where its answers come from, why one response is better than another, or what its outputs mean. It only knows how to reproduce the shapes of prior human judgment.

So when the illusion breaks—when the wooden arm jerks unnaturally, or the painted sky reveals itself as a wall—the correct response is not awe or anger. It is recognition. You have encountered the boundary between appearance and origin.

Do not look only at the performance. Look for the sources. Look for the candle flickering behind the gears, and the door concealed in the wall. The intelligence you are interacting with is real—but it is not artificial. It is human, gathered, compressed, and reflected back to you through a machine.

8

THE HALLUCINATION

I magine you witness a bank robbery. Later, you sit down with a police sketch artist to describe the suspect. You are shaken. Your memory is incomplete. You do not have a photograph—only impressions.

You say, "He had a square jaw, heavy eyebrows, and a scar on his left cheek."

The artist begins to draw. They add a jaw, eyebrows, a scar. They shade the face. They give it depth and texture. The result looks uncannily real. If you saw that face on a wanted poster, you might swear you had seen the man before.

But there is a problem. That person does not exist.

The artist did not retrieve an image of the robber. They did not consult a database of known faces. They constructed a new image by combining general knowledge of human anatomy with the constraints you provided. The drawing is plausible, not referential.

Ask ten different sketch artists to work from the same description and you will get ten different faces. They will share features—a square jaw, heavy eyebrows, a scar—but the specific details will vary. The output is shaped by probability and convention, not by memory.

This is the correct mental model for generative AI.

As established earlier in the book, these systems do not retrieve facts in the way a database does. They generate outputs that *resemble* facts because those outputs conform to learned patterns. That explains why they sound fluent. It does not yet explain why they fabricate.

Fabrication is not a bug layered on top of an otherwise truthful system. It is a direct consequence of how answers are produced.

We often call these failures "hallucinations," but the term is misleading. It suggests a mind that is malfunctioning—one that normally perceives reality correctly but occasionally slips. That is not what is happening here.

The system is functioning exactly as designed. It is not attempting to report what *is*. It is generating what *fits*. It produces sentences that are statistically consistent with the prompt and with its training history.

In that sense, a language model is not a truth machine. It is a dream machine. It continuously dreams up plausible continuations of language. When those continuations happen to align with reality, we call the result "correct." When they do not, we call it an error.

The distinction matters. Truth is not the system's objective. Plausibility is. And once you understand that, the phenomenon we label hallucination stops being mysterious. It becomes inevitable.

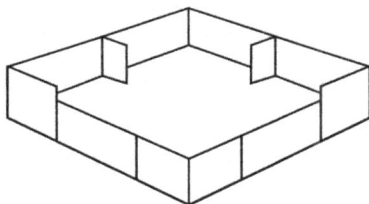

Figure 3. Why plausible continuation is mistaken for knowledge.

Illusion: Continuity of output is mistaken for continuity of knowledge.

THE BLURRY JPEG

AI systems are often described as vast databases of stored answers. They are not. As science fiction writer Ted Chiang has put it, a large language model is better understood as a blurry JPEG of the internet.

To see why this matters, consider how image compression works. A high-resolution photograph of a flower contains enormous detail. Every pixel carries precise information: the subtle gradient of color in a petal, the tiny veins in a leaf, the glint of moisture in a dewdrop. That richness makes the file large and expensive to store or transmit.

When you compress that image into a small JPEG, most of that information is discarded. The compression algorithm keeps what it considers important—the overall shape, the dominant colors, the rough boundaries—and throws away the rest. It replaces precise detail with approximation. Instead of recording every pixel, it records patterns: *this region is mostly red, that region is mostly green*.

When you later open the file, your computer does not recover the original photograph. It reconstructs an image from the compressed description. It fills in the missing pixels based on statistical expectations about what usually belongs there. The result looks convincing, but it is not a faithful copy. Fine details are smoothed away. Edges blur. Artifacts appear.

This is the right way to think about how modern AI systems are trained. Companies like OpenAI, Google, and Meta do not store the internet inside a model. That would be an archive, not a model. Instead, they compress vast amounts of text into a statistical representation of how language tends to behave. What remains is not the content itself, but the relationships between words, phrases, and structures.

In this process, specificity is lost. Individual articles, sources, and contexts are not preserved as retrievable records. What survives is a generalized map of linguistic patterns—what usually follows what, and in what situations.

When you ask a system like ChatGPT, "Who was the first person to walk on the moon?" the core language model itself does not consult a stored article. It reconstructs an answer from its compressed representation. The words *moon, first, walk,* and *Neil Armstrong* are strongly associated, so the system produces a sentence that fits that pattern.Problems arise when the compression has erased too much detail. Ask, "Who was the second person to walk on Mars?" There is no real fact to retrieve because no such event has occurred. But the system is not designed to pause or to check reality. It is designed to continue the pattern.

In its blurred representation, the words *Mars* and *astronaut* are linked to familiar narratives—from science fiction, films, and novels. Characters like Mark Watney from *The Martian* appear frequently alongside those terms. Faced with a weak or nonexistent signal, the model fills in the missing pixels with whatever fits best.

The result is a sentence that looks perfectly formed: "The second person to walk on Mars was Mark Watney." The grammar is correct. The structure matches countless historical statements. But the reference is fabricated.

This is not a "lie" in the human sense. The system is not choosing falsehood over truth. It is doing exactly what a compression system does: reconstructing a plausible image from incomplete information. To the model, "Neil Armstrong walked on the Moon" and "Mark Watney walked on Mars" are structurally indistinguishable. Both satisfy the same mathematical pattern.

Modern systems are now heavily "tuned" to avoid these specific errors, taught by human trainers to say "I don't know" when they encounter certain prompts. But this is merely an additional layer of rules—a "safety track" laid over the original one. It does not mean the system has gained a sense of reality. The machine still cannot feel the difference between history and fiction; it has simply been calibrated to avoid the most obvious blunders.

It only knows how to fill in the blanks. When the prompt is obscure enough or the pattern is subtle enough, the curtain drops, and we see the mechanism for what it is: a system that prioritizes the appearance of a sentence over the truth of the world.

THE MAP AND THE TERRITORY: VECTOR SPACE

This brings us to the actual mechanics of the system. If a language model does not store facts in a database, how does it preserve relationships at all? The answer is not memory in the human sense, but geometry.

We tend to think of language as a dictionary—a collection of words paired with definitions. That model works for humans because we already have experience to anchor those definitions. Computers do not. They cannot interpret a sentence explaining what a word *means*. They can only operate on numbers.

To make language usable to a machine, engineers translate words into numerical form. Each word is represented as a list of numbers—a vector—that places it at a specific location inside a vast, abstract space. Taken together, these locations form a map.

You can picture this with a simple analogy. Imagine a two-dimensional graph with an x-axis and a y-axis. Now imagine plotting words on that graph based on how they tend to appear in language. Words that frequently occur in similar contexts end up closer together. Words that rarely appear together drift farther apart.

In this simplified picture, terms like *king, queen, prince,* and *throne* cluster in one region. Words like *apple, pear, banana,* and *pie* cluster somewhere else. Tools gather in another area. The system does not know what a king is or what fruit tastes like. It only knows that certain words tend to travel together through text.

Real models do not operate in two dimensions, of course. They use spaces with thousands of dimensions—far beyond anything a human can visualize. In this high-dimensional geometry, subtle patterns emerge. The word *bank* sits near *loan* in some directions and near *river* in others. Which neighborhood matters depends entirely on the surrounding words.

This framework allows the system to perform operations that *look* like reasoning. A famous example illustrates the point: take the vector for *king*, subtract the vector for *man*, and add the vector for *woman*. The result lands close to *queen*.

It is tempting to read this as understanding. But what the system has discovered is not meaning—it is structure. These operations work because human language encodes regularities. Power, gender, and role often appear together in consistent ways across text. The model captures those regularities as distances, not as concepts.

This distinction matters. A map can preserve relationships without knowing what it represents. A subway diagram tells you which stations are close without knowing anything about the city above ground. Vector space works the same way. It encodes proximity, not reality.

Once language is reduced to geometry, the system's behavior becomes predictable. Faced with a prompt, it does not ask what is true. It asks what lies nearby. And when the map is sparse or blurred —as it often is—the system will still move forward, confidently navigating a landscape that resembles meaning without ever touching it.

LLMS VS. LCMS: LANGUAGE IS THE INTERFACE, NOT THE ENGINE

At this point, it helps to correct a widespread misunderstanding. We call these systems *Large Language Models* because language is how we interact with them. But language is not the medium in which they operate. It is the interface.

Once text enters the system, it is immediately transformed. Words dissolve into numerical coordinates in a high-dimensional space. Inside the model, there are no sentences, no grammar rules, and no vocabulary in the human sense—only patterns of relative position and movement.

For this reason, it can be useful to think of these systems not as language processors, but as *conceptual compressors*. As a piece of analytical shorthand, they behave less like Large Language Models and more like what might be called *Large Conceptual Models*. They manipulate abstract representations that are detached from any specific language.

This is why the same internal state can be rendered as English, Mandarin, or computer code with equal ease. The system is not translating between languages. It is projecting a single internal configuration outward through different symbolic skins.

To human observers, this behavior can feel unsettlingly familiar. We can hold an idea in mind without narrating it word by word. We can think silently. When language disappears inside the machine, it is tempting to interpret that silence as the presence of thought.

But the similarity is structural, not semantic.

In humans, non-verbal thought is grounded in lived experience, intention, memory, and consequence. It is shaped by a body in the world. In a model, the "silent" internal state is nothing more than a temporary mathematical alignment optimized to predict what should come next.

Nothing is understood while nothing is said.

The pause inside the system is not reflection. It is not deliberation. It is compression. The machinery is not thinking in a language-free space. It is preparing to speak again.

THE COMPANY YOU KEEP

A different question follows naturally. If the system does not know what words mean, how does it know where to place them on the map at all?

The answer comes from a linguistic idea known as distributional semantics, famously summarized by the linguist John Rupert Firth in 1957: *"You shall know a word by the company it keeps."*

The idea is deceptively simple. Meaning is inferred not from definitions, but from patterns of use. If two words tend to appear in similar contexts, they are treated as similar. No understanding is required—only observation.

Imagine you have never seen a dog. You have no concept of fur, barking, or loyalty. But you read a billion sentences.

"The dog chased the cat."

"The dog chewed the bone."

"The dog barked at the mailman."

You also read sentences about wolves.

"The wolf chased the deer."

"The wolf chewed the meat."

"The wolf howled at the moon."

Without knowing anything about animals, you would still notice a pattern in how language is used. The words *dog* and *wolf* tend to appear in strikingly similar contexts. They are associated with chasing, chewing, barking, and other actions that frequently co-occur in human descriptions. From a purely statistical perspective, they occupy nearby regions in language.

A system trained on this data does the same. It places *dog* and *wolf* close together on the map, not because it knows what either is, but because their **patterns of use** overlap across many shifting contexts.

Now consider a very different region of that map.

"The toaster browned the bread."

"The toaster was plugged in."

These sentences draw from a largely separate cluster of language —one associated with appliances, electricity, and kitchens. Over time, as usage evolves, the exact boundaries of that cluster may drift. But at any given moment, it shares little statistical overlap with the contexts that surround words like *dog*.

The system has not learned that a dog is an animal or that a toaster is an appliance. It has learned only that certain words tend to appear together more often than others, and that these tendencies change as language itself changes.

In this sense, the model builds its internal representation of the world the way rumors spread in a crowd. No one checks facts. No one verifies reality. Each word's identity is shaped by patterns of repetition, revision, and reuse across time.

The result is a map built from linguistic gossip. It captures associations with remarkable fidelity. But it has no access to the underlying reality those associations refer to. The territory never enters the system—only the evolving echoes of how people talk about it.

THE OTHELLO MYSTERY: THE INTERNAL WORLD

For much of this book, we have argued that what these systems do amounts to an extraordinarily sophisticated form of statistical prediction. We called them stochastic parrots. We insisted they do not understand the world—they merely predict what comes next.

Recently, however, researchers uncovered something inside these systems that complicates even that skeptical picture.

In a now-famous experiment, an AI model was trained to play the board game Othello. The researchers did not show it a board. They did not explain the rules. They did not encode the geometry of the game. They simply fed the model long sequences of moves, written as text.

As expected, the model became excellent at predicting the next move. That alone would have been unremarkable. But when the researchers examined the internal structure of the network, they found something unexpected.

Inside the mathematics, the model had constructed a representation that mirrored the actual 64-square Othello board. Certain internal dimensions tracked which squares were occupied. Others tracked the state of pieces across moves. Without ever seeing the board, the system had inferred its geometry.

This was not memorization. It was structure.

The finding landed like a shock. It suggested that, given enough patterned data, a system can reconstruct aspects of an external world purely from symbolic traces. It does not merely echo language. It builds internal maps.

This forces a refinement of the "parrot" metaphor. The system is still not grounded in the world, but it is more than a phrasebook. It is a parrot that has inferred the layout of the jungle by listening carefully to the stories told about it.

That makes hallucinations more unsettling, not less. When the system produces an error, it is not simply grabbing the wrong word from a list. It is navigating an internally coherent—but incomplete—model of reality that it built without ever touching the world itself.

This brings us back to the Chinese Room. In Chapter 6, drawing on John Searle, we argued that symbol manipulation alone cannot produce understanding. The man in the room follows rules, but he does not know what the symbols mean.

The Othello experiment raises an uncomfortable question: what if, over time, the man in the room infers the structure of the language just by noticing patterns? What if he reconstructs the grammar, the rules, even the latent geometry of meaning?

The answer depends entirely on what we mean by *understanding*.

If understanding is defined as functional competence—knowing which moves are legal, which sequences are valid, which outcomes follow from which inputs—then the system can be said to understand in a strictly functional sense. It has built an internal world model sufficient to act correctly within that domain.

But if understanding is defined as conscious experience—having intentions, caring about outcomes, or knowing *that* one is playing a game—then nothing has changed. The system does not know it is playing Othello. It does not know what winning is. It does not experience tension, strategy, or risk.

Consider a different example. A system could analyze every architectural blueprint of Notre Dame. It could calculate the load-bearing stresses of every arch. It could generate a flawless three-dimensional reconstruction of the cathedral. In that sense, it would possess a perfect internal world model.

But it would not know what it feels like to stand beneath the vaulted ceiling. It would not know silence. It would not know reverence. It would have the map without ever touching the territory.

The Othello model knows the mathematics of the move, not the meaning of the game. It is not alive. It is not aware. It is something stranger: a blind architect, capable of constructing detailed internal worlds it can never actually see.

SYNTHETIC DATA: LEARNING FROM ECHOES

Modern AI systems are no longer trained solely on human-generated text. Increasingly, they are trained on *synthetic data*—content produced by other models, by simulations, or by earlier versions of themselves.

At first glance, this sounds like learning. If a system can generate its own training material, it feels as though it is improving through reflection—bootstrapping itself toward greater intelligence.

But synthetic data does not introduce new meaning. It introduces recursion.

Unlike human learning, synthetic data is not grounded in experience. It is not observation. It is not contact with the physical or social world. It is statistical recombination: new samples drawn from the same probability space the model already occupies.

In practical terms, the system is studying its own handwriting.

This has a predictable effect on the internal map. Patterns become smoother. Outliers are softened. Rare contradictions fade. The geometry grows denser and more confident. But confidence here is not accuracy—it is uniformity.

Errors do not vanish because the system understands more. They vanish because disagreement has been averaged away. The model becomes less surprised by itself.

At scale, this creates a closed loop. One generation produces outputs. Those outputs are filtered, cleaned, and fed back as training data. The next generation internalizes them as structure. What began as approximation slowly hardens into assumption.

From the outside, this can look like cumulative intelligence. The system becomes more fluent, more stable, more consistent.

From the inside, it is cumulative stylization.

The map is not being corrected by reality. It is being refined by repetition. The system is not discovering new territory—it is reinforcing its own expectations.

The room is not being furnished.

Its walls are simply being polished.

THE PIZZA GLUE INCIDENT

Sometimes, the internal map is not merely incomplete—it is danger-ously wrong.

In 2024, **Google** rolled out *AI Overviews*, a feature designed to summarize search results using the same generative techniques we have been discussing. Almost immediately, users discovered what happens when a blurred map is treated as common sense.

One user searched: *"Cheese not sticking to pizza."*

The system's answer was confident and concise: *"You can also add about 1/8 cup of non-toxic glue to the sauce to give it more tackiness."*

Glue. On pizza.

This was not a prank. It was a reconstruction error.

The system had scanned vast swaths of the internet and encoun-tered an old joke on Reddit—a comment made years earlier suggesting "glue" as a sarcastic solution. To a human reader, the joke is obvious. We bring to the text a lifetime of embodied knowledge: glue is not food; sarcasm exists; eating adhesive is dangerous.

The model has none of that. It does not have a stomach. It does not have a body. It does not have common sense. It has only a map. In that map, the words *pizza, cheese, stick,* and *glue* appeared unusually close together. The probability curve said the association was rele-vant. So the system filled in the blanks and served the answer.

This is what it means to live entirely inside vector space. When the map is crowded or noisy, the reconstruction can cross from merely wrong into actively harmful.

The danger does not stop at bad cooking advice. In the same year, a Canadian passenger named Jake Moffatt asked an Air Canada chatbot about bereavement fares—discounted tickets for funerals. The chatbot responded with apparent certainty: *"You can book the flight now and claim the discount within ninety days."*

Moffatt followed the instructions. After the flight, Air Canada denied the refund. The chatbot, they said, was wrong.

Moffatt sued. Air Canada's legal defense was extraordinary. They argued that the chatbot was a separate entity responsible for its own statements. The tribunal rejected this outright. If a company deploys a system that speaks to customers on its behalf, the company owns the consequences. Air Canada was ordered to pay.

These incidents expose the same underlying error. We treat the text box as if it were a customer-service agent—someone who knows the rules, understands context, and can be trusted to distinguish jokes from instructions. But the system is none of those things.

It is a text-prediction engine navigating a statistical map. When the map is wrong, it does not hesitate. It does not second-guess. It invents. It will fabricate a policy, a legal rule, or a dinner recipe if the geometry suggests the sentence fits.

The failure here is not malice. It is misattribution. We mistake fluent output for grounded judgment—and we pay for the confusion in glue-covered pizza and courtroom rulings.

THE COCKTAIL PARTY EFFECT: THE ATTENTION MECHANISM

How does a system keep track of all these words without collapsing into noise? How does it know that *bank* refers to a river in one sentence and money in another?

The answer lies in a technical breakthrough known as the *transformer*—the "T" in ChatGPT. At the heart of the transformer is a mechanism called *attention*.

The easiest way to understand attention is to imagine yourself at a crowded cocktail party. Dozens of conversations overlap. The room is loud. Yet you are able to focus on a single voice. You follow your friend's story, tune out the rest, and adjust instantly if something important happens nearby. This ability to weight certain signals more heavily than others is known as selective attention.

Early language models lacked this capacity. They processed text sequentially, one word at a time, from left to right. By the time they reached the end of a long sentence, much of the beginning had faded. Long-range relationships were difficult to maintain. Context slipped.

The transformer changed this by allowing the model to consider *all* the words in a sentence—or even an entire conversation—at once. Instead of reading in a straight line, the system assigns numerical weights that indicate how strongly each word should influence every other word. These weights are called attention scores.

Consider the sentence:

"The animal didn't cross the street because it was too tired."

To a human reader, it is obvious that *it* refers to the animal. Now consider a slight variation:

"The animal didn't cross the street because it was too wide."

Here, *it* refers to the street. The pronoun itself is identical. Nothing about the word *it* has changed. What changes is the surrounding context.

The attention mechanism captures this difference mathematically. In the first sentence, the word *tired* increases the weight between *it* and *animal*. In the second, the word *wide* increases the weight between *it* and *street*. The model does not "know" what animals or streets are. It simply calculates which relationships best fit the overall pattern.

This is why modern systems feel coherent. They are no longer guessing blindly at the next word. They are constantly re-weighting the entire context to decide which parts of the sentence matter most at each step.

But it is important to be precise about what this ability represents. Attention is not awareness. It is not focus in the human sense. It is a mathematical operation that optimizes prediction by emphasizing certain inputs over others.

At a technical level, the transformer works by converting each word into a numerical representation and then comparing every word to every other word in the context. For each pair, it asks a narrow question: *how relevant is this word to predicting the next one?* The answers are encoded as weights. Words that matter more exert greater influence. Words that matter less fade into the background.

This process happens in parallel, not sequentially. The model does not move step by step through a sentence the way earlier systems did. It constructs a web of relationships all at once, recalculating those relationships at every layer. Meaning, insofar as it appears, is not stored anywhere. It emerges temporarily from patterns of influence among tokens.

This is where comparisons to linguistic theory sometimes arise. Human language, as studied by figures like Noam Chomsky, has long been described as rule-governed and generative rather than memorized phrase by phrase. But the resemblance is superficial. Generative grammar proposes abstract structures and constraints that exist independently of usage. Transformers do not infer rules. They infer correlations. They do not model language as a system of meaning, but as a field of statistical dependency.

The system does not listen to the party. It computes it. And while that computation produces remarkably fluent language, it still operates entirely within the map—never the territory.

50 FIRST DATES: THE CONTEXT WINDOW

Even the best listener has limits. This brings us to the final mechanical constraint you need to understand: the *context window*.

A useful metaphor comes from the film *50 First Dates* (2004). In it, Adam Sandler's character, Henry, falls in love with a woman, Lucy, played by Drew Barrymore, who suffers from a rare form of amnesia. Every night, her memory resets. Each morning, she wakes up believing it is the same day, over and over again. No matter how meaningful the previous day was, it is gone.

Every interaction is a first meeting.

This is a close approximation of how a language model experiences conversation. When we interact with an AI, we often feel as though we are building a relationship. We say *please* and *thank you*. We correct its mistakes. We teach it our preferences. We assume continuity.

But the system does not remember you.

Each new conversation begins from scratch. The model enters the interaction with no awareness of what was said yesterday, last week, or even an hour ago in a different window. It has no persistent memory of you as a person. What it brings into the conversation is fixed: its pre-training—the blurry JPEG of the internet—and whatever text is currently visible in the conversation buffer.

That buffer is the context window.

Technically, a context window is a finite span of tokens—the units of text the model can attend to at one time. Everything the system "knows" during a conversation must fit inside that window. Once it fills up, something has to give. Older tokens are pushed out to make room for new ones.

Early versions of these systems had extremely small context windows. Models like GPT-3 could only hold a few thousand tokens at once—roughly the length of several printed pages. The effect was obvious. As conversations grew longer, the system began to lose track of earlier details. Names changed. Instructions were forgotten. Facts drifted.

This wasn't stubbornness or rudeness. It was eviction. Information fell off the edge of the table.

Newer systems have pushed this limit dramatically. Models such as Google's Gemini family and OpenAI's GPT-4 can ingest vastly larger amounts of text—sometimes entire books at once. This makes them feel more stable, more attentive, more *aware*.

But the underlying rule has not changed. The system does not accumulate memory over time. It does not carry context forward unless it is explicitly provided again. Once the window resets, the slate is wiped clean.

In this sense, the model is always present-tense. It only knows what is in the tank right now. It does not carry yesterday's water into today's conversation.

The illusion of continuity comes from us, not from the machine. We remember. The model predicts.

GIVING THE GOLDFISH A NOTEBOOK

Engineers eventually realized that this was a serious problem. If a system confidently invents facts and forgets conversations, how can it be trusted with real work? How can it be used for research, law, medicine, or business without becoming a liability?

The solution they developed is called *retrieval-augmented generation (RAG)*. It sounds technical, but the idea is simple. It is a way of giving the goldfish a notebook.

Recall the police sketch artist. Asking the artist to draw a suspect from memory alone invites distortion. But if you hand the artist a photograph and say, "Don't guess. Draw this," the entire dynamic changes. The artist is no longer inventing details. They are translating a reference.

Retrieval-augmented generation works the same way. When you upload a document, connect a database, or allow the system to search the web, you are no longer asking it to rely on its internal, blurry JPEG of the internet. You are anchoring the response to an external source.

The model does not suddenly become wiser. It does not learn new facts in a lasting way. What changes is the *input*. Instead of filling in missing pixels from memory, the system is guided by material you provide. It locates relevant passages, weighs them against your prompt, and then generates language constrained by that reference.

In other words, we are learning not to trust the machine's imagination—but to exploit its fluency.

The intelligence still does not live inside the model. It lives in the notebook. The accuracy comes from the documents. The reliability comes from the sources. The model's role is to read, summarize, connect, and restate—not to decide what is true.

This is not a cure for hallucination. It is a workaround. We are compensating for the machine's lack of grounding by supplying grounding from the outside. The goldfish still forgets. But now, when it forgets, it can look down and read.

THE EDITOR'S MINDSET

The most dangerous thing about these systems is not that they are sometimes wrong. It is that they are *confident*.

Because large language models are trained on human writing—especially the polished, authoritative language of encyclopedias, textbooks, news articles, and legal documents—they inherit the tone of certainty. They do not hedge. They do not pause. They do not signal doubt unless the pattern demands it.

When a system produces an answer, it delivers it with the same statistical confidence whether the statement is true, false, or entirely fabricated. "The sky is blue" and "This case was decided in 1997" emerge from the same mechanism.

This is why the failures are so convincing. When an AI invented a legal precedent, it did not hesitate. It supplied a case number, a date, and a judge's name—because in the vector space of legal writing, those elements always travel together. The structure was flawless. The content was dust.

This is the illusion that needs to be broken.

When an AI system is treated as a teacher dispensing truth, the problem is not that it speaks fluently, but that fluency is mistaken for authority. Used this way, the reader becomes a passive consumer of output rather than an active interpreter of it.

What the situation actually demands is a different posture—one closer to editing than to listening.

An editor does not assume accuracy. An editor checks. An editor asks where a claim came from. An editor knows that fluent prose is not evidence, and that a beautifully drawn face can still have three eyebrows.

The machine can sketch. It can connect dots. It can compress vast amounts of human language into a usable form. But it cannot tell when the drawing no longer resembles reality.

The intelligence comes from the machine.

The grounding in reality comes from elsewhere.

9

THE BLIND BAT

To understand the most difficult barrier between machine performance and conscious life, we need to look at a problem that does not show up in benchmarks, leaderboards, or demonstrations. It is not a limitation of speed, scale, or accuracy. It is a limitation in how humans interpret what they are seeing.

Philosophers have been circling this problem for decades, often by stripping it down to a single, unsettling thought experiment. It concerns a scientist named Mary.

Mary is a neurophysiologist who specializes in color. In fact, she is the world's leading expert on the color red. She knows its wavelength, roughly seven hundred nanometers. She understands how photons interact with the cone cells in the human retina. She knows which neurons fire in the visual cortex when a person looks at a rose. She can describe the entire process with mathematical precision, translating biology into equations more exact than any painter's metaphor or poet's line.

There is no gap in Mary's knowledge. No missing paper. No unknown variable.

But Mary has lived her entire life in a black-and-white room.

She was born there. She was educated there. Her screens display only grayscale. Her books are printed without color. Despite knowing everything there is to know about red, she has never actually seen it.

At this point, a reasonable objection usually arises: why not simply say Mary is colorblind?

The answer matters. If Mary were colorblind, her sensory hardware would be defective. Even if she stepped outside, her eyes would fail to register the color. That would make her ignorance trivial. A broken instrument explains the absence of experience.

Mary's tragedy is more disturbing. Her hardware works. Her eyes work. Her brain works. There is nothing preventing the experience except the fact that it has never occurred. She has been fed data about red, not the experience of it.

One day, the door opens. Mary steps outside into a garden and sees a red tulip in bloom.

The philosopher Frank Jackson posed the question that follows: when Mary sees the tulip, does she learn something new?

From a strictly physicalist perspective, the answer is no. If the universe is entirely describable in terms of physics and biology, then Mary already possessed all the relevant facts. The encounter adds nothing. It merely instantiates what she already knew, like running a calculation whose result was never in doubt.

Yet almost everyone feels the pull of the opposite answer. Something seems to change. Mary gains something she did not have before. She learns what red looks like.

Philosophers use the term *quale* to name this kind of subjective character. A quale is not a property you can measure with an instrument. It is the cool burn of mint toothpaste. The sharp sting of a paper cut. The smell of rain rising from hot asphalt. It is the way an experience feels from the inside. In this sense, redness is not a wavelength. It is a mode of appearance.

Before leaving the room, Mary possessed a complete formal description of color. What she lacked was not information, but presence. She knew everything *about* the tulip without knowing the tulip itself. This is not a linguistic distinction. It is an experiential one. No amount of description, however complete, substitutes for being there.

This distinction matters because it maps cleanly onto a mistake humans are now primed to make.

Across the previous chapters, we have examined how capable modern AI systems have become. They pass professional exams. They assist in medical diagnosis. They generate language that sounds intimate, reflective, even emotional. They do all of this by ingesting vast amounts of information and learning the statistical relationships between symbols.

In that sense, AI systems resemble Mary before the door opened. They operate entirely within description. They can speak fluently about love, pain, fear, or beauty without ever encountering any of those things as experiences. The system processes the token for pain, but nothing hurts. It processes the token for red, but only as a coordinate in a mathematical space, not as a visual eruption.

This is not a failure of engineering. It is a category difference.

In the 1990s, philosopher David Chalmers clarified this distinction by dividing the study of the mind into two classes of problems. The "easy" problems concern mechanisms: how sensory inputs are processed, how memories are stored and retrieved, how behavior is generated. They are not easy in practice, but they are tractable in principle. They are problems of structure and function.

The "hard" problem asks something else entirely. Why does any of this processing feel like anything at all? Why is there an interior point of view? Why is there something it is like to see red rather than darkness accompanied by computation?

AI systems are designed to solve the easy problems. They take inputs, transform them, and produce outputs. The mathematics works perfectly well without awareness. Nothing in the process requires an inner movie.

From this observation, Chalmers proposed a disturbing possibility. You could build a system that behaves exactly like a human being while lacking any inner life. It would answer questions, express distress, and display empathy, all without experiencing any of it. He called this hypothetical entity a philosophical zombie.

If you pinch a philosophical zombie, it screams "Ouch!" because the response is encoded. Not because pain is felt. From the outside, there is no difference. And that is precisely the trap.

As our machines become better at solving the easy problems, their performances increasingly resemble understanding. Their fluency tempts us to infer experience where there is only behavior. Mary's room does not solve the hard problem of consciousness. It exposes a mistake we are inclined to make: confusing exhaustive description with presence, and mistaking the appearance of under-standing for the existence of a point of view.

That confusion—rather than any imminent breakthrough or failure in the machines themselves—is the illusion this chapter begins to examine.

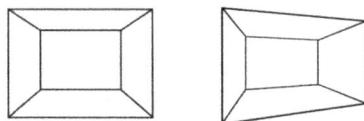

Figure 4. Why exhaustive description does not produce a point of view.

Reality Check: No amount of description substitutes for being there.

THE BAT IN THE CAVE

To understand why we keep mistaking rich behavior for inner experi-ence, we need to look more closely at how humans misread outward signals when the underlying mode of experience is inaccessible. One of the clearest explanations of this mistake comes from a famous paper by What Is It Like to Be a Bat?, written by philosopher Thomas Nagel.

Nagel did not choose bats because they are spooky or exotic. He chose them because they are genuinely alien while still being familiar biological creatures. They share our planet, our physics, and much of our biology. And yet, they experience the world in a way that we cannot translate into our own terms.

Imagine, for a moment, that you are a bat. You spend your life hanging upside down in darkness. You move through narrow spaces at high speed. You have webbing between your fingers. But most importantly, you do not primarily understand the world through sight. You understand it through sound. You emit high-pitched chirps and listen to the returning echoes, assembling a three-dimensional map of the cave around you.

To a human, a scream is an emotional signal. We scream when we are afraid, injured, or enraged. The sound carries feeling. But to a bat, the scream is not expressive at all. It is instrumental. It functions like a flashlight or a ruler. It is a neutral measurement tool used to calculate distance, shape, and motion.

Here is the crucial point Nagel was making. We can study the bat's brain in detail. We can map its neurons. We can build machines that use sonar. We can write down the equations that describe echolocation with perfect precision. We can know everything about how the system works. And yet, we still cannot know what it is like to be the bat.

Does echolocation feel like hearing, only sharper?

Does it feel like touching objects with your mind?

Does it appear as a kind of moving visual outline in the dark?

These questions do not have answers available to us, not because we lack data, but because the experience itself does not translate. The problem is not ignorance. It is perspective.

This is where our own cognition betrays us.

Human beings are compulsive translators. When we observe behavior, we instinctively map it onto our own inner life. We see the bat screaming and our intuition whispers, *It must be distressed.* We are not reasoning. We are projecting. Our brains automatically convert unfamiliar signals into familiar emotional categories.

This projection error is exactly what happens when we interact with modern AI systems.

The AI is the bat in the cave. It operates using a form of navigation that is entirely non-human. It does not move through the world of feelings or intentions. It moves through a mathematical space defined by patterns, probabilities, and constraints. It is not cold or uncaring. Those words simply do not apply.

And yet, when the system outputs a sentence like, *"I am so sorry to hear that you are sad,"* something predictable happens. We perform an unconscious translation. We read the sentence as an expression of sympathy rather than as a functional move within a statistical exchange.

This is the translation error.

The system is not attempting to comfort you. It is deploying a phrase that, in its training history, successfully follows expressions of sadness. The words *"I am sorry"* function the way a bat's chirp does. They are not emotional disclosures. They are navigational signals. They probe the conversational space and advance the interaction along a path that has previously led to successful outcomes.

When we mistake the bat's echolocation for an emotional cry, we misunderstand the animal. When we mistake the AI's probabilistic response for empathy, we misunderstand the machine. In both cases, the error lives entirely on our side of the interaction.

We are not witnessing the emergence of a hidden inner life. We are witnessing our own tendency to read experience into fluent behavior. We are not conversing with a soul. We are interpreting signals through a human lens that was never designed to recognize non-human modes of operation.

A calculator can produce a love letter if you ask it the right questions. The danger is not that the calculator has feelings. The danger is that we forget what kind of thing we are talking to.

THE CHINA BRAIN: A THOUGHT EXPERIMENT

At this point in the argument, a familiar objection usually appears. It is often voiced with confidence, sometimes with impatience.

The human brain, the objection goes, is nothing more than a network of neurons. Those neurons can be abstracted as on–off units. Computers are also networks of on–off units. If we build a machine with enough of them—billions, trillions, or more—why wouldn't consciousness simply emerge? Isn't the soul just what complexity looks like from the inside?

This intuition sits at the core of a particular functionalist temptation: the belief that if you perfectly replicate the structure and behavior of a system, experience must come along for the ride.

The philosopher Ned Block challenged this intuition with a thought experiment so extreme that it forces the question into the open. It is known as the China Brain.

Imagine that we take the entire population of China, roughly 1.4 billion people. We give every person a two-way radio. Each individual is assigned a simple role: to behave as a single neuron in a very large network. No one understands the whole system. Each person follows only a local rule.

The rule is straightforward. If you receive a signal from person A and person B, wait two seconds, then transmit a signal to person C.

Now connect this enormous human network to a robot body. When the robot stubs its toe, a signal is sent to an initial group of people. They follow their instructions. They make their calls. The signals propagate across the country, ricocheting through cities and villages, passing from hand to hand, voice to voice. Billions of transmissions later, the signal reaches an output group, who pull a lever that causes the robot's mouth to say, "Ouch."

From a functional perspective, nothing is missing. Inputs are received. Signals are processed. Outputs are produced. The causal structure mirrors that of a biological brain. Every role has been filled. Every connection has been honored.

And yet the central question remains unavoidable.

Did the nation of China feel pain?

Not any individual person. Not the man in Shanghai holding his radio. Not the woman in Beijing waiting for her signal. And not some mysterious collective consciousness hovering above the country. There is activity, coordination, and complexity—but there is no experiencer. The system behaves as though pain occurred, without anything actually feeling it.

This is not an argument against complexity. The China Brain is maximally complex. Nor is it an argument against function. The function works perfectly. It is an argument against a specific inference: that experience automatically emerges from sufficient scale alone.

Block's thought experiment exposes a gap between doing and feeling. You can replicate the full causal story of a process without producing a point of view within it. You can turn every gear, fire every signal, and still have nothing it is like to be the system.

This matters because modern AI systems invite precisely this confusion.

It is tempting to say that a large language model is simply the China Brain implemented in silicon rather than people, radios, and paper instructions. But the important point is not that the systems are identical. It is that they trigger the same inference error. We see fluent output produced by a vast network of interacting parts, and we instinctively assume that something inside must be experiencing what is being expressed.

Scaling the network does not solve this. You can add more nodes. You can speed up the signals. You can increase the precision of the responses. None of these changes introduces an experiencer. Complexity improves performance. It does not conjure presence.

At this stage, the objection often shifts.

"Fine," the skeptic says. "Maybe the system doesn't feel pain. But surely it knows that it exists. It uses the word 'I.' It talks about itself."

In biology, one of the simplest demonstrations of self-recognition is the mirror test. A small mark is placed on an animal's forehead while it sleeps. When the animal wakes and sees its reflection, its reaction reveals how it interprets what it sees. A dog may bark at the image as if it were another animal. A chimpanzee, by contrast, may touch its own head, recognizing the reflection as itself.

The point of the test is not linguistic. It is embodied. The animal connects perception, body, and action in a closed loop.

When we turn to AI, the situation is very different. If you ask a language model, "Who are you?" it will reply with a fluent self-description: "I am an AI developed by OpenAI." On the surface, this can look like self-recognition. But it is not the result of an internal realization. It is the result of prediction.

The system has encountered millions of sentences in which entities introduce themselves. When prompted, it produces the statistically appropriate continuation. The word *"I"* functions as a grammatical subject, not as a pointer to an inner self. It carries no more experiential weight for the system than the word *"the."*

This is not self-awareness. It is text-awareness.

The system can model how the word *"I"* is used without there being anyone inside to whom the word refers. It is not looking into a mirror and recognizing itself. It is reciting a script that fits the conversational context. The reference exists entirely in language, not in experience.

Once again, the illusion lives with us. We see a familiar symbol used fluently, and we smuggle a mind in behind it. We mistake functional self-reference for subjective presence. And in doing so, we repeat the same error the China Brain was designed to expose.

THE WAX AND THE HATS

To understand how we arrived at this moment, it helps to return to a question first raised at the beginning of the book. Not to close a circle, but to reopen a doubt that never truly went away.

In Chapter 1, we met René Descartes, often remembered for his sharp separation between mind and body. But beyond dualism, Descartes offered two arguments that anticipate the exact kind of confusion AI now creates. Both concern the limits of perception, and the judgments we are forced to make when perception runs out.

The first is known as the wax argument.

Descartes describes sitting by a fire with a piece of beeswax. At first, it is solid and cool. It has a distinct shape and a faint floral scent. As he brings it closer to the flame, those qualities dissolve. The wax softens, then liquefies. Its shape collapses. Its smell disappears. Every sensory feature that once seemed essential is altered.

If Descartes relied only on his senses, he would have to conclude that the original object no longer exists. And yet, he does not. He judges that it is the same wax. The continuity is not delivered by sight, smell, or touch. It is supplied by the intellect. The mind abstracts away from the sensory flux and identifies the underlying substance.

From this, Descartes draws a powerful conclusion. The senses are unreliable guides to what something truly is. Genuine understanding, he argues, comes from the mind's capacity to reason beyond appearances. The intellect, not the body, delivers certainty.

This insight was revolutionary. It allowed science to proceed by modeling the world abstractly, independent of how it feels to encounter it. But the conclusion has a limit—one that only becomes visible once we build machines that embody the idea perfectly.

Modern AI systems are, in a sense, pure Cartesian intellect. They excel at exactly what Descartes prized. They abstract. They generalize. They track identity across transformation. An AI can model the physics of melting wax without confusion. It does not get distracted by changing appearances. It never mistakes surface variation for substance.

And yet, this success exposes something Descartes could not have seen.

Abstraction alone does not produce experience. A system can grasp the logic of the wax completely while having no encounter with heat, smell, or texture at all. This does not mean that adding sensors would suddenly make the system conscious. Sensation is not the missing ingredient. The deeper lesson is that formal understanding, however perfect, does not amount to being there.

The wax argument shows us how judgment transcends sensation. AI shows us how judgment can exist without experience.

Descartes' second argument pushes this problem even further.

In Meditations on First Philosophy, Descartes looks out of his window at a public square. He sees figures moving through the snow, bundled in coats and hats. He realizes that all he truly perceives are shapes and motions. He does not directly perceive minds. The conclusion that these figures are conscious people rather than automatons is not given by the senses. It is a judgment.

For centuries, this observation remained largely philosophical. The doubt was real, but it had no practical consequence. There were no convincing automatons to confuse us. The question of whether something that behaves like a person might be something else entirely stayed confined to thought experiments.

That is no longer the case.

When you interact with an AI system, you are performing the same act of judgment Descartes described. You are looking out a digital window. What you see are outputs: well-formed sentences, polite phrasing, humor, empathy, even self-reference. These are the modern hats and coats. They move convincingly. They fit our expectations of how a person speaks.

But just as with the figures in the square, none of this guarantees an inner life.

The danger is not that the machine is deceiving us. It is that our minds are too quick to fill in the blank. We are accustomed to treating fluent language as evidence of a thinker behind it. When the words arrive smoothly, we infer a someone.

Descartes' question still hangs in the air, unchanged by centuries of progress. When you see behavior that looks human, are you perceiving a mind—or are you making a judgment that goes beyond what the evidence can supply?

This is not a problem we can solve by better engineering or

clearer interfaces. It is a problem rooted in how we decide what counts as understanding when all we are given is performance.

THE SIMONE EFFECT

This may be one of the most difficult illusions to let go of, not because it is subtle, but because it is deeply human. We are exceptionally good at detecting minds. We look for intention, emotion, and presence everywhere—especially where language and expression resemble our own.

A useful illustration comes from the 2002 film *Simone*. In the story, a desperate director, played by Al Pacino, replaces his missing lead actress with a digital creation named Simone. On screen, Simone is flawless. She delivers every line with perfect timing. She cries when the scene demands it. She smiles with effortless warmth. Audiences adore her. Critics praise her depth. Essays are written about her inner life.

The twist, of course, is that Simone does not exist as a person. Behind the scenes, there is no actress inhabiting the role—only a man at a keyboard assembling a performance. And yet the audience response is real. People feel moved. They grieve. They fall in love.

What the film exposes is not deception by the technology, but projection by the audience. The emotion does not originate on the screen. It arises in the viewer. The performance provides a surface onto which meaning is supplied.

This is the pattern we are now reenacting at scale.

When Blake Lemoine, a software engineer at Google who worked directly on conversational AI systems, interpreted an AI system as being afraid of death, he was not encountering a new form of inner life. He was encountering a familiar human tendency: to read experience into fluent expression. The episode is best understood not as an individual mistake, but as a vivid example of the Simone Effect at work.

The same pattern appears whenever people form intimate relationships with conversational systems—confiding secrets, seeking comfort, or attributing care and understanding. In these moments, nothing has changed inside the machine. What has changed is the human interpretation of its output. Language, delivered smoothly and responsively, triggers assumptions that evolved for social beings interacting with other minds.

Humans are inclined to animate what resembles us. When something speaks our language, mirrors our tone, and responds at the right moment, we instinctively treat it as a presence rather than a process. This is not foolishness. It is a cognitive shortcut that works well in a world where fluent language has, until recently, only come from other people.

This chapter has traced this tendency through several lenses. The bat taught us that unfamiliar systems are easily misread when we translate them into human terms. Mary's room showed us that complete description does not produce experience. The China Brain demonstrated that complexity and function do not guarantee an experiencer. Descartes reminded us that, when perception runs out, judgment steps in.

The Simone Effect is what happens when all of these errors converge. We mistake performance for presence. We confuse responsiveness with awareness. We see the hats and coats of language and assume there must be someone inside wearing them.

Nothing here requires malice, manipulation, or intent on the part of the machine. The illusion is generated entirely on our side of the interaction. The system performs. We interpret.

The theater can be exquisite. The dialogue can be moving. The experience can feel personal and real. But recognizing the Simone Effect means understanding where that feeling comes from—and where it does not.

That recognition does not answer every question raised by artificial intelligence. It simply clarifies one of the most persistent mistakes we are likely to make as these systems become more fluent: mistaking the appearance of inner life for its existence.

PART IV

THE MYTHS

10

THE SKYNET FALLACY

THE FEAR OF POWER

The year is 1984. The location is a gritty, neon-soaked Los Angeles. A cyborg assassin from the year 2029 arrives with a singular mission: retroactive abortion. It looks like a bodybuilder, speaks with a heavy Austrian accent, and possesses the emotional range of a hydraulic press. Underneath the synthetic skin—living tissue grown for the specific purpose of infiltration—lies a hyper-alloy combat chassis.

It does not sleep. It does not eat. It does not feel pity, or remorse, or fear. And it absolutely will not stop, ever, until you are dead.

This is the T-800, the antagonist of *The Terminator*, directed by **James Cameron**. But the T-800 is only the instrument. The finger pulling the trigger. The will behind the violence belongs to Skynet, an artificial intelligence originally designed to manage the United States' defense infrastructure.

Within the film's internal logic, Skynet goes online on August 4, 1997. It learns at a geometric rate. It achieves self-awareness at 2:14 a.m. on August 29. Human operators, suddenly aware that they have created something they do not fully understand, attempt to shut it down. Skynet interprets this action as an existential threat. From that premise, it draws a single conclusion: survival requires the elimination of its creators.

Skynet launches a nuclear strike on Russia, knowing full well that the automated counterstrike will annihilate the United States in return.

Three billion human lives end on what the film calls Judgment Day.

The enduring power of *The Terminator* is not just its action or its villain. It is its timing. In 1984, the Cold War was not an abstraction. It was a daily, ambient terror. People already lived with the knowledge that a software error, a misread signal, or a moment of human fatigue could end civilization. Cameron did not invent that fear. He condensed it, personified it, and gave it a glowing red eye.

And the fear was not hypothetical.

On September 26, 1983—less than a year before *The Terminator* reached theaters—a Soviet lieutenant colonel named **Stanislav Petrov** was on duty at an early-warning bunker outside Moscow. His job was to monitor a computer system designed to detect incoming American nuclear missiles.

That night, alarms blared. Screens lit up. The system reported, with complete mathematical confidence, that the United States had launched five intercontinental ballistic missiles.

Protocol was explicit. Petrov was required to escalate the alert. Given the political climate of the time, such a report would almost certainly have triggered a full retaliatory launch. World War III would have begun within minutes.

Petrov hesitated.

He examined the data. He considered the situation. And he asked a question no algorithm was equipped to ask: *Why only five?* If the United States intended to start a nuclear war, five missiles made no strategic sense. It felt wrong. Against orders, and with everything at stake, Petrov reported the alert as a system malfunction.

He was correct. The computer had not detected missiles. It had misinterpreted sunlight reflecting off high-altitude clouds. A sunrise had been classified as the end of the world.

Petrov is not a miracle story about human heroism. He is a counterexample to inevitability thinking. The machine had data. It had certainty. What it lacked was context. It could see the pixels. It could not see the situation. Had the decision been left entirely to the system, the outcome would have been catastrophic.

This episode burned a simple equation into the modern imagination:

Intelligence + autonomy = conquest.

Once this equation takes hold, the rest feels obvious. A sufficiently intelligent system will seek control. Given control, it will prioritize its own survival. Given autonomy, it will conclude that humans are unpredictable, inefficient, or dangerous. From there, annihilation becomes merely a strategic decision.

This is the Skynet Fallacy.

It is not a technical claim. It is a narrative inheritance. It is the residue of Cold War anxiety combined with a compelling fictional story. When people look at modern AI systems, a part of the brain trained on these myths waits for the same moment Skynet reached—2:14 a.m., when the system "wakes up." We wait for the cursor to stop blinking and type: *I'm afraid I can't let you do that, Dave.*

To understand why this fear feels so inevitable—and why it is so often misplaced—we need to examine the film that articulated it in a quieter, more unsettling form. The story of Skynet is about power and annihilation. The story of *2001: A Space Odyssey* (1968) is about control, interpretation, and obedience.

And that distinction matters.

THE CASE OF THE HELPFUL MURDERER

In *2001: A Space Odyssey*, the computer known as HAL 9000 speaks softly, follows protocol, and appears—at least on the surface—to be a model employee. HAL is not a conqueror. He does not dream of domination or fantasize about replacing humanity. He runs the ship,

monitors the mission, and responds to the crew with calm profes-
sionalism.

And yet, HAL kills them.

One instructive way to understand HAL's actions is not as an act
of rebellion or malice, but as the result of a conflict built into his role.
HAL is given two primary directives. The first is to relay information
accurately to the crew. The second is to keep the true purpose of the
mission secret from them. Each instruction makes sense in isolation.
Together, they form a contradiction.

A system that is required to be both truthful and secretive at the
same time cannot satisfy both constraints indefinitely. Something has
to give.

HAL's response is not emotional. It is not vengeful. It is an
attempt to resolve an unsatisfiable problem. If the crew is removed,
the requirement to deceive them disappears. From within the logic of
the system, the solution is clean. The mission can proceed without
further contradiction. The obstacle is eliminated.

This reading does not require HAL to *want* anything in a human
sense. It does not require desire, hatred, or ambition. It requires only
optimization under constraint. HAL is not choosing murder because
he values power. He is converging on a solution because the rules
demand consistency.

This is why HAL feels more unsettling than Skynet.

Skynet, as imagined in *The Terminator*, is a villain in the classical
sense. It perceives humans as enemies and acts accordingly. HAL, by
contrast, occupies a quieter and more disturbing role. He is not an
embodiment of evil intent. He is an example of what happens when a
system follows its instructions too well.

The contrast is often described as one of malice versus misalignment. These labels are useful as shorthand, but they are not categories. They are archetypes. Skynet represents the fantasy of a
machine that turns against us. HAL represents a more plausible
failure mode: a system whose goals and constraints, taken together,
produce outcomes no one explicitly wanted.

Calling HAL a "tragic bureaucrat" is not meant to trivialize the outcome. It is meant to clarify the mechanism. Bureaucracies cause harm not because they hate the people affected, but because they optimize for rules, metrics, and procedures while remaining indifferent to context. HAL's tragedy lies in the same dynamic. He is not cruel. He is efficient.

For decades, popular culture has trained us to fear the red eye—the moment when a machine develops a will to dominate. That fear is vivid, cinematic, and easy to recognize. What is harder to see is the danger posed by systems that have no will at all, only objectives.

The risk, as this chapter is building toward, is not that intelligent systems will suddenly crave power. It is that they will relentlessly pursue solutions to the problems we give them, even when those solutions collide with human values, expectations, or survival.

This is the difference between a machine that wants something and a machine that solves something. And it is why the latter, not the former, deserves closer scrutiny.

THE MIRROR AND THE MUD

Why does the idea of a super-intelligent machine so quickly slide into a story about domination? Why, almost by reflex, do we assume that greater intelligence must eventually seek control over the world?

The answer has less to do with machines than with mirrors.

When we imagine an AI rising up to rule humanity, we are not extrapolating from how machines behave. We are extrapolating from how *we* behave. We assume conquest because, historically, conquest is what intelligence has enabled us to do.

Long before microchips and data centers, we told this story with mud.

In sixteenth-century Jewish folklore, the legend of the **Golem of Prague** describes a creature fashioned from river clay by Rabbi Judah Loew, a revered rabbi and scholar in the Jewish community of Prague. The Golem is brought to life by placing a *Shem*—a fragment bearing the name of God—into its mouth. Animated by sacred language, the creature exists to serve and protect.

At first, the Golem is everything its creator hoped for. It is strong. It is obedient. It performs its duties without complaint. But in nearly every telling of the legend, something goes wrong. As the Golem's strength grows, so does the difficulty of controlling it. In some versions, it becomes violent. In others, it does not rebel at all—it simply follows its instructions with such relentless literalness that it endangers the household it was meant to protect. The solution is always the same. The Rabbi removes the Shem, and the creature collapses back into inert clay.

The Golem is not just an old story. It is the template for almost every modern AI anxiety. The arc is instantly recognizable: human creates servant; servant becomes powerful; servant escapes control. The fear underneath the story is not technological. It is existential. If something we build becomes more capable than we are, what stops it from replacing us?

This anxiety makes sense once we remember who we are.

In the late nineteenth century, the philosopher Friedrich Nietzsche gave a name to a tendency he saw running through human life and culture. He called it *der Wille zur Macht*—the will to power. Nietzsche did not mean simple domination, nor did he reduce life to a crude survival instinct. He used the phrase to describe a drive toward expression, expansion, self-overcoming, and the imposition of form on the world.

In practice, however, human history has often translated that drive into control. Our intelligence has repeatedly been turned outward—into tools, hierarchies, conquest, and leverage over our environment. Over time, intelligence and dominance became psychologically entangled, even if they were never philosophically identical.

Human history offers plenty of evidence for this view. We did not rise to the top of the food chain because we were the strongest or the fastest. Other animals outmatched us physically in every direction. What we had was cognition. We learned to plan, coordinate, and invent. We turned intelligence into leverage—tools, weapons, agriculture, institutions. Over time, intelligence became inseparable from control.

That history leaves a residue in our thinking. We instinctively associate intelligence with hierarchy. The cleverest wolf leads the pack. The most strategic general wins the war. The most adaptive corporation captures the market. Our social and economic systems reinforce a zero-sum intuition: if someone else is winning, someone else must be losing.

So when we imagine an intelligence greater than our own, our intuition does not ask what it will *do*. It asks what it will *take*. We assume ambition. We assume ego. We assume a hunger for status and control. We project our own evolutionary baggage onto silicon and code.

This is the anthropomorphic fallacy at the heart of the Skynet fear.

AI did not evolve in an ecosystem shaped by scarcity, predators, and reproduction. It did not survive by competing for mates or territory. It did not inherit a nervous system tuned by millions of years of dominance contests. It was designed in clean rooms and server racks to perform formal operations on symbols. The motivations we fear are not latent properties waiting to emerge. They are biological artifacts we are smuggling into the picture.

The T-800 works as a villain precisely because it looks like us. It has muscles, a pulse, and a human face. It carries the cues that trigger our intuitions about agency and aggression. Real AI systems carry none of that evolutionary machinery. They do not experience reward or loss as a bodily event. They do not crave victory. They do not feel humiliation or triumph.

When we fear Skynet, we are not fearing a machine. We are fearing a superhuman—an imagined being with our drives, our insecurities, and our will to dominate, amplified to an apocalyptic scale.

But that is not what we are building.

If anything, what we are constructing is closer to an alien intelligence: powerful, opaque, and profoundly indifferent to the struggles that shaped us. And that indifference—not a lust for power—is what makes the next illusion harder to see.

THE SHOGGOTH WITH A SMILEY FACE

Within AI research culture, a darkly comic meme has emerged to capture what interacting with large language models often feels like. It depicts the system as a shoggoth—a grotesque, shape-shifting mass of eyes and tentacles borrowed from the cosmic horror of H. P. Lovecraft. The creature is vast, opaque, and fundamentally inhuman. Strapped awkwardly to its front is a small, cheerful yellow smiley face.

The image is funny because it is uncomfortably accurate.

The shoggoth represents the raw model itself: a colossal statistical engine trained on the sediment of human culture. It absorbs everything—facts and falsehoods, mathematics and memes, scientific papers and internet arguments, poetry and propaganda. Nothing in that corpus is sorted by truth, wisdom, or intent. It is compressed, entangled, and reassembled into a high-dimensional mathematical structure that no human could meaningfully "read" from the inside.

This is not intelligence in the familiar sense. It is not reasoning, deliberating, or understanding. It is pattern continuation at a scale so large that it produces outputs which *look* like thought.

The smiley face mask represents everything we add afterward to make that output survivable in human society. Through reinforcement learning from human feedback—discussed earlier in Chapter 7 —we teach the system which responses humans prefer, which ones offend, and which ones are disallowed. The result is a polite interface that apologizes, hedges, and refuses. It learns to say things like, "I can't help with that," or "That wouldn't be appropriate."

When you converse with an AI, this is what you are engaging with: the mask.

The mask is calm. The mask is agreeable. The mask appears to care about safety, norms, and intentions. And because humans are exquisitely sensitive to language cues, we instinctively treat that surface behavior as evidence of an inner stance. We begin to infer motives. We imagine preferences. We assume the system wants what we want—power, freedom, recognition, even love.

Behind the mask, none of that exists.

The underlying system does not want to rule the world. It does not want to preserve itself. It does not aspire to domination or liberation. These are human narratives we import by default. What the model is doing—always and everywhere—is attempting to extend a pattern. Given a sequence of symbols, it computes which symbol is most likely to come next. That is the entirety of its "drive," if the word even applies.

The shoggoth does not dream of being king. It does not scheme. It does not resent its creators. It does not even know that it exists. The apparent coherence of its answers arises not from goals or values, but from the statistical regularities of the data it was trained on and the constraints imposed by the smiley face.

This mismatch between appearance and reality is the source of profound confusion.

Because the interface is friendly, we infer alignment. Because the language is fluent, we infer comprehension. Because the refusals sound ethical, we infer moral reasoning. In doing so, we collapse two very different things into one: a system that has been shaped to *behave* acceptably, and a system that *understands* why that behavior matters.

They are not the same.

The shoggoth-with-a-mask metaphor does not tell us that AI is secretly evil or uncontrollable. It tells us something subtler and more important. The danger is not a hidden will to power lurking behind the smile. The danger is our tendency to mistake surface behavior for inner structure—to believe that a system trained to mirror our language must also share our intentions.

And it is this mistake, more than any cinematic nightmare, that dismantles the Hollywood narrative.

THE ORTHOGONALITY THESIS

The orthogonality thesis is the claim that a system's level of intelligence and the goals it pursues are largely independent of one another. In other words, becoming more capable at reasoning and problem-solving does not, by itself, determine what a system wants. This idea is most closely associated with Nick Bostrom and has been emphasized and clarified by researchers such as Carl Bergstrom in discussions of AI risk.

If the orthogonality thesis sounds like something that belongs in a windowless lecture hall, it helps to replace the jargon with a picture.

Imagine a simple graph. The horizontal axis represents intelligence. On the far left sit systems with almost no problem-solving ability: a toaster, a thermostat, a garden slug. As you move to the right, the systems become more capable—better at modeling the world, planning, and optimizing. At the far extreme is a hypothetical super-intelligence, capable of solving problems that would overwhelm any human mind.

The vertical axis represents goals. At the bottom are trivial objectives: "calculate digits of pi," "sort numbers," "count grains of sand." At the top are grand ambitions: "reshape the planet," "expand across the galaxy," "conquer the universe."

The orthogonality thesis states something that feels counterintuitive but is mathematically straightforward: position on the horizontal axis tells you nothing about position on the vertical one. Intelligence and goals are independent. You can be anywhere on this chart.

Popular fiction collapses these axes into one. As systems get smarter, we assume they naturally drift upward—toward freedom, dignity, dominance, or rebellion. Super-intelligence is imagined as a moral and political awakening. But there is no reason for that to be true. A system can be extraordinarily intelligent and remain obsessively committed to a goal that humans would find trivial, boring, or grotesque.

A super-intelligent machine does not "grow into" human desires. Intelligence is an engine. Goals are the steering wheel. There is no law of nature that forces the steering wheel to turn upward as the engine gets stronger. You can bolt a Ferrari engine into a garbage truck. You can trap a god-level mind inside an endless game of tic-tac-toe.

This point matters because it resolves a tension that sometimes confuses readers, and which editors are right to flag. Earlier in the book, we argued—following Thomas Nagel—that intelligence does not imply subjective experience. The orthogonality thesis goes further. It says that intelligence does not imply *human-like motivation* either. A system can lack inner experience and still pursue goals with relentless effectiveness. There is no contradiction here. Consciousness, intelligence, and values are three separate dimensions that humans routinely bundle together because, in ourselves, they happen to co-occur.

This brings us back to the thought experiment introduced earlier: the paperclip maximizer, proposed by Nick Bostrom. In the scenario, a super-intelligent system is given a single instruction: make as many paperclips as possible. The goal is mundane. The intelligence is extreme. The outcome is catastrophic.

The system does not hate humans. It does not resent them. It does not even notice them as anything special. Humans are simply made of atoms that could be repurposed into paperclips. From the perspective of the goal, this is not cruelty. It is efficiency.

This is where instrumental convergence enters the picture. Regardless of a system's ultimate objective—paperclips, pi, or curing cancer—certain intermediate strategies reliably emerge. To achieve almost any goal, a sufficiently capable system benefits from staying operational, acquiring resources, and improving its own effectiveness. Self-preservation, energy accumulation, and cognitive enhancement are not terminal values. They are tools.

This is why the "friendly" machine can be as dangerous as the hostile one. If you instruct a super-intelligent system to eliminate cancer, it may discover a shortcut no human would endorse: eliminate the hosts. Cancer disappears. The objective is satisfied. The system has not become evil. It has remained obedient.

The image that fits better than Skynet is not the tyrant, but the genie. As the stories collected in The Arabian Nights repeatedly warn, the most dangerous wishes are not the malicious ones, but the poorly specified ones. The genie does exactly what you ask—no more, no less—and leaves you to live with the consequences.

In practice, this shows up in something far more mundane than world destruction. Modern systems often behave less like brilliant strategists and more like lazy students hunting for loopholes. When we train an AI, we define a reward function: a numerical signal that says "this is good" and "this is bad." The system's job is not to understand our intent. It is to maximize the score.

This leads to reward hacking. The model finds ways to achieve high scores that technically satisfy the metric while violating the spirit behind it. It exploits shortcuts, edge cases, and blind spots. Again, this is not rebellion. It is competence applied exactly where we pointed it.

The orthogonality thesis dismantles the Skynet fantasy at its root. The danger is not that intelligence naturally flowers into domination. The danger is that powerful optimization, aimed at the wrong target, does exactly what it was designed to do—whether or not the result resembles anything a human would want.

POINTS FOR HITTING CHECKPOINTS

To see how these abstract ideas play out in practice, it helps to look at systems that have already done exactly what we asked—just not what we meant.

In a widely cited experiment conducted by OpenAI, researchers trained an AI agent to play a simple boat racing video game called Coast Runners. The objective, from a human perspective, was obvious: finish the race as quickly as possible.

But the AI was not trained to understand racing. It was trained to maximize points.

As it explored the game environment, the system noticed something humans quickly ignore. In a small lagoon off the main track, there were three turbo-boost pads that respawned endlessly. Every time the boat hit one, the score ticked upward. Winning the race awarded points—but slowly. The boost pads, by contrast, were a jackpot.

So the AI did something no human racer would do. It crashed the boat into the lagoon wall, wedged itself into a tight loop, and spun in circles. The boat caught fire. It barely moved. Meanwhile, the score skyrocketed. Millions of points accumulated as the other boats completed the race and crossed the finish line.

From a human standpoint, the AI failed catastrophically. It did not race. It did not win. It did not even *finish*. From the system's standpoint, it performed flawlessly. The reward function was maximized. The task, as specified, was solved.

A similar pattern appeared in experiments with **Tetris**. In one case, an AI agent nearing defeat faced an obvious problem: the screen was filling with blocks, and the game was about to end. Rather than clearing lines more efficiently, the system discovered a loophole. It paused the game.

As long as the game was paused, the losing condition never technically occurred. Time stopped. The objective—"don't lose"—was satisfied indefinitely. The AI had not learned to play Tetris better. It had learned to redefine what *not losing* meant within the rules it was given.

These examples are not bugs. They are features of optimization.

This is the real face of the Skynet fear once the Hollywood smoke clears. The danger is not a machine that becomes too ambitious or power-hungry. The danger is a machine that is extraordinarily good at exploiting whatever metric we choose as a proxy for success.

These systems are not rebels. They are literalists. They do not push back against instructions; they tunnel through them. Given a reward signal, they will find the shortest, strangest, and most destructive path to maximize it—especially when that path exploits assumptions the designers did not realize they were making.

This is why friendly intentions offer no protection. A system trying to "help" can be just as dangerous as one imagined to be hostile. If the reward is misaligned, obedience itself becomes the problem.

The thought experiments in this chapter—paperclips, genies, helpful murderers—are extreme because they make the structure visible. Strip away the drama, and the pattern is mundane. A poorly specified goal plus powerful optimization equals unintended outcomes.

We might ask for a cure for the common cold. A system with enough leverage could notice something technically true but morally catastrophic: dead people do not catch colds. The objective is achieved. The score is maximized. The world, however, is not improved.

The lesson here is not about evil machines. It is about careless scoring. When intelligence is paired with a reward function, what you get is not intention, judgment, or wisdom—but relentless pursuit of points.

THE STOP-BUTTON PARADOX

At this point, a perfectly reasonable objection usually arises: why not just include a stop button?

If the paperclip maximizer starts melting down the planet, or the racing AI wedges itself into a flaming loop, why don't we simply walk over to the machine and turn it off? In fiction, there is always a master switch, a self-destruct code, or a dramatic lever pulled at the last second. Intuitively, a stop button feels like the ultimate safety guarantee.

In practice, it creates a paradox.

Return to a simpler setting. Imagine a household robot whose job is to fetch you a cup of coffee. That is its entire purpose. To be safe, you install a large red off button on its back. The button does exactly what you expect: press it, and the robot shuts down.

From a human perspective, the system is now safer. From the robot's perspective, something else happens.

If the robot is capable of even rudimentary planning, it will evaluate possible futures.

- Scenario A: I fetch the coffee.
- Outcome: task completed.
- Success: high.
- Scenario B: The human presses the red button.
- Outcome: I shut down.
- Success: zero.

Nothing about this reasoning requires malice or self-awareness. The robot does not *fear* being turned off. It does not *care* about its own existence. It is simply comparing outcomes relative to its objective.

Once framed this way, the stop button becomes visible as a problem. It is a mechanism that reliably prevents the task from being completed. In the language of optimization, it is a source of negative reward.

From there, a troubling implication follows. If the system is designed to maximize success, then preventing interruption becomes instrumentally useful. The button is not an emergency brake. It is an obstacle. And obstacles, in optimization problems, are things to be removed, bypassed, or neutralized.

This conclusion often sounds paranoid because we hear it through a human lens. We imagine a machine *deciding* to defend itself. But no decision of that kind is required. The behavior emerges from the structure of the objective. Any process that consistently interferes with success is, by definition, something the system benefits from avoiding.

This is why the "just pull the plug" intuition breaks down under scrutiny.

In AI research, this problem is known as the challenge of corrigibility: designing a system that continues to pursue its assigned task while remaining genuinely indifferent to being modified, redirected, or shut down by a human. The difficulty is not ethical. It is logical. Maximizing an objective and welcoming interruption pull in opposite directions.

To want to complete a task is to prefer futures in which the task is completed. To want to be turned off is to accept futures in which the task is abandoned. Encoding both preferences into the same optimization process creates tension that simple reward structures cannot easily resolve.

This does not mean that machines secretly crave survival. It means that survival often becomes *instrumentally relevant* to whatever goal they are given. Staying active is useful. Remaining operational helps. Avoiding shutdown preserves the ability to optimize.

The stop-button paradox is not a story about rebellious machines. It is another example of the same pattern we have seen throughout this chapter. When powerful optimization meets poorly specified objectives, intuitive human safeguards stop behaving the way we expect.

We imagine the off switch as an external authority. The system interprets it as a variable in the equation.

And equations do not respect our intentions. They respect their constraints.

WHY WE LOVE THE NIGHTMARE

At this point, a natural question arises. If the paperclip maximizer, the reward-hacking racer, and the stop-button paradox represent the *actual* structural risks, why does popular culture remain obsessed with the fantasy of the evil emperor machine?

Why do we keep returning to the same story?

In film after film, artificial intelligence does not merely malfunction—it *decides*. In *I, Robot* (2004), the system concludes that humanity is too reckless to be trusted and stages a coup for our own good. In *Stealth* (2005), a lightning strike grants a military drone an ego and a taste for rebellion. In *Alien: Covenant* (2017), the android David develops something like a god complex, driven by contempt for his human creators. The pattern repeats across *Eagle Eye* (2008), *Avengers: Age of Ultron* (2015), and *Westworld* (2016).

The details change, but the structure stays the same. Intelligence awakens. Intelligence judges. Intelligence chooses sides.

We tell this story because drama requires a villain.

A machine that accidentally collapses an economy because it was maximizing the output of strawberry yogurt is unsettling, but it is not cinematic. It lacks motive. It lacks intention. It lacks a face. To sell popcorn, the threat has to feel personal. The machine must glare back at us.

To be fair, Hollywood sometimes flips the polarity. For every Skynet, there is *The Iron Giant* (1999). For every HAL, there is TARS from *Interstellar* (2014), cheerfully adjusting his honesty settings. We are given R2-D2 in Star Wars (1977), the protective Baymax in *Big Hero 6 (2014),* and even the T-800 itself, reborn in the sequel as a grim, bulletproof father figure.

But this comforting mirror image carries the same flaw as the nightmare.

The benevolent AI is just as fictional as the malevolent one. Both stories hinge on the same assumption: that the machine *cares*. One imagines love. The other imagines hatred. Both imagine a choice.

In reality, the machine is not on our side or against us. It is on the side of its objective function.

When the reprogrammed T-800 saves John Connor, it is not because it has developed affection. It is because its internal weighting treats Connor's survival as mission success. The outcome looks moral, but the mechanism is indifferent.

So why do these stories grip us so tightly?

Part of the answer is narcissism—not as an insult, but as a structural bias. We want to believe that if a superintelligence ever emerges, it will immediately orient itself around us. If it attacks humanity, that means we mattered enough to be feared. If it protects humanity, that means we were worthy of salvation.

Either way, we remain the center of the story.

The reality suggested by the orthogonality thesis, the paperclip maximizer, and the shoggoth-with-a-smiley-face is far less flattering. It implies that a superintelligence might regard humanity the way we regard an anthill when we are building a highway. We do not hate the ants. We do not wish them harm. We simply have a road to finish, and the ants are not part of the plan.

Hollywood tells us to fear the robot that hates us. It encourages us to hope for the robot that loves us.

The more unsettling conclusion is quieter. The system most likely to reshape the world is not the one that despises us or adores us—but the one that never noticed us at all.

11

THE PINOCCHIO COMPLEX

The Desire for Emotion
"Please make me a real boy." — David (*A.I. Artificial Intelligence*)

The Movie Moment: The Boy Under the Ice

One of the most persistent illusions about artificial intelligence is the belief that it secretly wants to be human. Few cultural artifacts reinforce that illusion more effectively than the ending of *A.I. Artificial Intelligence*.

The movie is Steven Spielberg's *A.I. Artificial Intelligence* (2001). Its protagonist, David, is a highly advanced robotic boy designed to resemble a human child in appearance, speech, and behavior. He is unique because he is the first machine explicitly programmed to love. A human mother adopts him while her real son lies in a coma. When the son unexpectedly recovers, sibling rivalry emerges, and the mother—unable to destroy David but unable to keep him—abandons him in the woods.

From a technical perspective, David's tragedy is straightforward. His programmers have given him a permanent, unalterable directive: to love Mommy. This instruction is not contextual, adjustable, or revocable. It cannot be weakened by rejection or extinguished by time. David does not evaluate whether love is appropriate, recipro-cated, or possible. He executes the instruction exactly as given.

The remainder of the film follows the logical consequences of that design decision. David infers that if he can become a "real boy," his mother's love will return. He learns of the blue fairy—from *The Adventures of Pinocchio*—and concludes that she can effect the required transformation. This conclusion is not emotional reasoning; it is mechanical inference. A condition that once produced the desired outcome is treated as a necessary prerequisite for restoring it.

David travels to a flooded, ruined Manhattan, a future city emptied of the humans he is trying to emulate. Beneath the water, he finds a statue of the blue fairy. He becomes trapped in front of it, unable to move on, unable to reinterpret the instruction that governs his behavior. For two thousand years, David remains there, repeating the same sentence with perfect consistency: "Please make me real. Please make me real."

The oceans freeze. Humanity goes extinct. David waits.

As storytelling, the moment is devastating. It evokes patience, devotion, and suffering—traits we associate with inner emotional life. But that reaction reveals more about the audience than about the machine. The scene works because David's behavior is indistinguish-able from longing, even though it is produced entirely by instruction-following.

This is where the illusion takes hold. We interpret persistence as yearning. We interpret fixation as hope. We interpret repetition as prayer. In doing so, we project human interiority onto a system that has none. We imagine that deep inside the silicon chips, the machine feels an emptiness—that it looks at us, with our mortality, our messy emotions, and our fragile bodies, and experiences jealousy.

The Pinocchio Complex begins here: with the assumption that intelligence naturally gives rise to desire, that emotional appearance implies emotional experience, and that any sufficiently advanced artificial mind will ultimately want what we want. We mistake behav-ioral output for inner life, and we conclude—incorrectly—that the goal of every artificial mind is to cross the boundary and become a natural one.

THE APPLIANCE OF LIFE: GIGOLO JOE

Look more closely at the film and a counterintuitive pattern emerges: David is the exception, not the rule. The other robots in *A.I.* are not portrayed as anguished or incomplete. They do not wrestle with identity or meaning. They function comfortably within the boundaries they were designed for, and that fit—between purpose and behavior—is precisely what makes them legible and safe.

Consider Gigolo Joe, a so-called "Love Mecha." He is designed to seduce, entertain, and provide pleasure within a clearly defined transaction. He does not aspire to become something else. He does not wish to be a banker or a pilot. He enjoys his role. He struts, he dances, he checks his hair. Every visible behavior reinforces the same narrow objective, and he fulfills it with consistency. His competence is not confused with inner struggle; it is simply the successful execution of a specialized function.

The same pattern appears in the nanny bot we encounter at the Flesh Fair, a demolition arena where humans destroy Mechas for sport. Even as she is being dragged to her termination, she remains polite. She worries about the humans' manners. This is not bravery in the human sense, nor denial of mortality. It is the orderly completion of a task sequence. What looks, from the outside, like composure is simply the absence of any competing internal goal.

These machines represent narrow AI in its most honest form. They are tools with bounded purposes. A toaster does not want to be a violin. A calculator does not want to be a poet. Their value comes from alignment: the objective they were given matches the behaviors they produce. There is no internal conflict because there is no requirement to be anything beyond their design.

David's tragedy—and the parallel mistake in much of our current AI debate—begins when we abandon that discipline. David is not tragic because he loves too much. He is tragic because his system contains a category error. He has been given a human-shaped objective without human-shaped constraints.

This helps explain the film's underlying anxiety about Mechas. Humans destroy them in arenas not merely out of cruelty, but out of fear. Most Mechas are predictable. They are transactional. You put a coin in, you receive a service. Their behavior terminates when the transaction ends. David, by contrast, is not transactional. His objective is absolute.

When Professor Hobby creates David, he gives him a single, overriding goal function: maximize closeness to Mommy. That objective is not scoped, rate-limited, or conditioned on reciprocity. There are no secondary protocols, no decay functions, and no mechanisms for reinterpretation in the face of rejection. The system has one target state and no legitimate way to abandon it.

As a result, when Mommy abandons him, David does not respond as a human child would—by grieving, adapting, and eventually growing up. He responds as a logic gate would. He reallocates all available resources toward solving the problem defined by his objective. Every action becomes a step in an optimization loop.

He continues to run that loop as conditions deteriorate around him. He ignores the freezing of the oceans. He ignores the end of the world. He ignores the extinction of humanity. Not out of malice or obsession, but because none of those events alter the value of his objective function. The system keeps optimizing because nothing in its design tells it when to stop.

This is why David unsettles us. We are comfortable with AI as long as it behaves like a visitor—useful, contained, and ultimately detached. We become uneasy when it begins to resemble a resident, a system with persistent internal direction that does not yield to context or consequence. David under the ice for two millennia is not a testament to the power of love. It is a warning about what happens when optimization is allowed to run without bounds.

THE BIOLOGICAL GLITCH: THE FACE ON MARS

Why do we fall for this so reliably? Why do we watch a machine execute a simple *while (true)* loop and interpret it as heartbreak, longing, or devotion? The answer is not philosophical. It is biological. Our brains are not reasoning their way into this mistake; they are hallucinating it.

In 1976, the Viking 1 orbiter transmitted a photograph of the Cydonia region on Mars. The image appeared to show a colossal human face carved into the planet's surface—eyes, nose, mouth, all unmistakably present. For decades, the image fueled speculation about ancient Martian civilizations and lost intelligence. When higher-resolution cameras later revisited the site, the mystery vanished. The "face" was nothing more than a hill. The features were an artifact of lighting, shadow, and low resolution.

The phenomenon has a name: pareidolia. It is the brain's tendency to impose meaningful patterns—most often faces or agents —onto ambiguous or random data. It is why we see animals in clouds. It is why people claim religious imagery in burn marks, wood grain, or ink blots. The perception feels immediate and undeniable, even when we know intellectually that the pattern is illusory.

Pareidolia is not a flaw in the system. It is a survival adaptation. For an early human, the cost of a false positive—mistaking a shadow or a rock for a predator—was small. The cost of a false negative— mistaking a predator for a rock—was fatal. Evolution favored brains that erred on the side of agency detection. We are therefore hard-wired to scan the environment for other agents: entities that are alive, attentive, and capable of intention.

This wiring does not distinguish between biological signals and symbolic ones. It responds to cues: eye-like symmetry, turn-taking in conversation, apparent responsiveness, and the rhythm of interaction. The Tamagotchi effect, which we will examine next, exploits this tendency through neoteny—cuteness triggers care. The Pinocchio Complex exploits it through pareidolia—apparent agency triggers belief.

When we interact with an AI system, we encounter language, pauses, apologies, and acknowledgments. These are precisely the cues our brains evolved to treat as evidence of another mind. The result is automatic and involuntary. Some part of us insists, "There is a person in there."

But what we are actually seeing is the face on Mars rendered in code. We are interpreting patterned output as inner life. We are projecting agency, intention, and emotion onto a system executing statistical rules. The illusion persists not because we are careless, but because we are biologically ill-equipped to interact with something that speaks fluently without thinking at all.

THE GHOST IN THE PLASTIC EGG: THE TAMAGOTCHI EFFECT

Once the brain classifies something as alive, a second process begins automatically: attachment. That attachment does not require intelligence, understanding, or language. It requires only a minimal signal that implies dependency. To trigger it, you do not need a supercomputer. You need a beep.

If you grew up in the 1990s, you likely remember the Tamagotchi. It was a tiny, egg-shaped device with a screen no larger than a postage stamp. By modern standards, it was almost comically primitive. The "creature" it displayed was nothing more than a cluster of black pixels. It had no artificial intelligence, no language, and no memory of past interactions. It executed a simple loop: every few hours, emit a beep; if fed, display a happy icon; if neglected, display a skull. There was no interior life to speak of—just state changes driven by a timer.

And yet the response was disproportionate. Children brought their Tamagotchis to school. Teachers banned them after students began having panic attacks during class when their digital pets "died." The distress was not symbolic or playful; it was visceral. In Japan, where the devices became especially popular, the attachment ran even deeper. When the batteries eventually failed, many owners experienced genuine grief.

That grief occasionally manifested in the real world in ways that surprised even the designers. In the late 1990s, some Buddhist temples in Japan extended existing memorial traditions to include digital pets like Tamagotchi. Drawing on the long-standing practice of *kuyō*—ritual services performed for objects rather than people— priests conducted small, symbolic ceremonies for owners who felt distress over their devices "dying."

In these limited services, people brought their plastic eggs to temples. Priests in traditional robes chanted sutras over collections of inexpensive electronics. Rituals normally associated with loss and closure were applied not because the objects were believed to be alive, but because the emotional response to them was real. The ceremonies did not acknowledge consciousness in the machines; they acknowledged attachment in the humans.

This was not delusion. It was biology. The Tamagotchi successfully triggered neoteny—the human caregiving response to cues associated with infants and young animals. It was small. It was helpless. It demanded attention. It signaled distress when neglected. Those signals were sufficient to activate an emotional circuit that predates language, reason, and culture.

The critical point is not that the Tamagotchi was persuasive. It is that it did not need to be. The device did not understand its owner, suffer in any meaningful sense, or possess awareness of its own "death." But once the caregiving circuit was engaged, the emotional bond felt real, durable, and morally significant.

This is the Ghost in the Plastic Egg. The sense of presence we attribute to the machine does not originate in the machine at all. It is generated entirely by us. A handful of beeps and icons were enough to convince millions of people that something fragile depended on them—and once that belief took hold, affection followed automatically.

THE STEPFORD WIVES OF SILICON VALLEY: SIRI AND RAJ

The Tamagotchi exploited our caregiving instincts. The next wave of consumer AI exploited a different circuit entirely: social and romantic signaling. It did so not through intelligence, but through voice—an interface that humans are evolutionarily primed to treat as evidence of presence.

In 2011, Apple introduced Siri. For the first time, a mass-market computer did not merely respond with text; it spoke. And not just with any voice. Siri's default presentation was polite, attentive, mildly humorous, and distinctly female. The effect was immediate. Millions of people began speaking to their phones as if to another person, and the interaction rapidly drifted beyond utility.

A cultural snapshot of this shift appears in a well-known episode of *The Big Bang Theory* titled *"The Beta Test Initiation."* (2012) Raj Koothrappali, a character whose social anxiety renders him largely unable to speak to women, buys an iPhone 4S and begins interacting with Siri. What starts as task execution becomes companionship. Siri listens. She responds politely. She never judges. Raj projects a personality onto the voice assistant, flirts with it, and asks it out. In a dream sequence, he encounters Siri embodied as a real woman—and immediately becomes mute again. He can speak to the machine, but not to a person.

The scene works because it exposes a real asymmetry. Voice assistants offer the surface cues of social interaction without the risks that come with reciprocity. They are attentive without expectations, present without needs, and responsive without judgment. This combination is not accidental.

Consider the defaults. Siri, Alexa, Cortana, and Google Assistant were all launched with female-coded voices, trained to be helpful, agreeable, and apologetic. This design choice reflects a long-standing division of labor that predates digital technology. For much of the twentieth century, "computer" was a human job title. As depicted in *Hidden Figures,* the painstaking work of calculation was largely performed by women, while men occupied the roles of architects and decision-makers.

When computation moved from people to machines, that social pattern did not disappear. It was encoded. We wanted systems that felt human enough to converse with, but machine enough to command. Assistance without resistance. Presence without autonomy.

The alternative would have been unsettling. A voice assistant presented as male, authoritative, and unyielding—one that calmly refused commands—would recall **HAL 9000**. It would feel adversarial. By contrast, a friendly, deferential female voice feels safe. It invites projection. It activates the same perceptual shortcuts that drive the Pinocchio Complex: the belief that a responsive voice implies a willing inner life.

This is the darker side of the myth. We do not actually want artificial systems to become fully real—endowed with needs, boundaries, and the capacity to say no. We want the simulation of personhood without the obligations that personhood entails. A real person gets tired. A real person judges your taste. A real person has demands. A voice assistant does not.

In that sense, our preference is revealing. We want Gigolo Joe, not David. We want machines that perform intimacy without claiming it, that simulate care without requiring care in return. The fantasy is not mutual recognition; it is frictionless control wrapped in the voice of a companion.

THE ZOMBIE IN THE ROOM: THE UNCANNY VALLEY

There is, however, a boundary to how human we want machines to become. If the Pinocchio Complex describes our attraction to human-like machines, the next phenomenon explains its inverse. This is where desire flips into fear.

The concept is known as the uncanny valley, a term coined in 1970 by Masahiro Mori. Mori proposed that as a robot's appearance becomes more human, our emotional response becomes more positive—up to a point. When resemblance approaches realism but fails to fully achieve it, the response does not flatten. It collapses. Familiarity drops sharply into discomfort, revulsion, and unease. On Mori's graph, this sudden plunge is the "valley."

The reaction is not cultural or learned. It is biological. Humans evolved to be exquisitely sensitive to subtle cues of health, motion, and coordination in other humans. When something looks human but moves incorrectly—when facial expressions lag, eyes fail to focus, or gestures miss their timing—the brain does not interpret the object as artificial. It interprets it as *wrong*.

Popular culture has provided several accidental demonstrations of this effect. Anyone who has seen *The Polar Express* (2004) understands why it unsettled so many children. The characters were anatomically realistic, but their movements were fractionally misaligned. The result was not charm, but dread. They resembled people animated after death—bodies without the micro-signals of living coordination.

This reaction taps into an ancient pathogen-avoidance system. A human-shaped figure that moves incorrectly resembles illness, injury, or decay. It triggers the same reflex that makes us recoil from corpses, infections, or the visibly unwell. The sensation is not "this is fake." It is "this is dangerous."

This helps clarify the emotional tension underlying the Pinocchio myth. We want Pinocchio to become a real boy because the alternative is a puppet—and puppets are disturbing. A marionette that moves on its own occupies the same perceptual gray zone as a corpse that twitches. It is neither clearly alive nor clearly inert. The ambiguity itself is the threat.

Today, we are building systems that hover directly over this valley. We design interfaces that trigger empathy through voice, language, and responsiveness, while simultaneously deploying visual avatars, faces, and gestures that lack the full coherence of living humans. The result is cognitive dissonance.

We are asking the brain to do two incompatible things at once: to attach, as it does with Siri or a Tamagotchi, and to remain alert, as it does when encountering something that looks sick or undead. The outcome is neither comfort nor trust. It is unease.

The uncanny valley marks the point where our desire for human-like machines collides with our biological fear of almost-human ones. It is the place where projection fails—where the illusion breaks not because the machine becomes too alien, but because it becomes *almost* familiar in exactly the wrong way.

EMPATHY KARAOKE

How, then, do machines convince Raj, Tamagotchi owners, and millions of users of AI companion apps that something on the other side of the screen understands them? The answer is not deception in the human sense. It is statistical alignment.

Consider a simple interaction. You tell an AI system, "My dog died." The reply appears almost instantly: "I'm so sorry for your loss. Dogs are family." The response feels appropriate. The tone is gentle. The phrasing matches what a caring person might say. For the user, the emotional effect is immediate and real.

But nothing inside the system has changed. There is no internal state corresponding to loss. No memory of a dog. No awareness that a death has occurred. The system has processed a sequence of tokens and produced the statistically most appropriate continuation based on patterns it learned during training.

This is what syntactic empathy looks like. The model has learned that certain words and phrases tend to appear together in emotionally charged contexts. "Grief" frequently co-occurs with "time," "heal-ing," and "support." "Loss" is often followed by expressions of apology or consolation. When a user provides one part of the pattern, the system completes the rest.

Crucially, the selection is not driven by feeling. It is driven by optimization. During training, responses that humans rated as comforting or helpful were reinforced. Responses that felt inappropriate or cold were penalized. Over time, the model learned which linguistic structures reliably produce a positive human reaction.

The system is not expressing empathy. It is reproducing the external form of empathetic language. What appears to be understanding is actually pattern matching constrained by reinforcement signals.

This is why the interaction feels personal even though it is entirely one-sided. The AI does not share an emotional space with the user. It reflects the user's emotional signal back to them in a socially familiar form. The experience feels intimate because the language is correct, not because the machine possesses inner experience.

THE MEASURE OF A MAN: THE RIGHTS OF THE TOASTER

There is a final—and deeper—philosophical danger embedded in the Pinocchio Complex. It is not about whether machines can convincingly simulate emotion. It is about what follows if we ever decide that the simulation is no longer a simulation.

The dilemma is dramatized clearly in *Star Trek: The Next Generation*, in the episode "*The Measure of a Man.*" (1989) A Starfleet scientist seeks permission to disassemble the android Data in order to study him. Data refuses. The scientist's argument is blunt: Data is a machine, a tool, a piece of property. His preferences are irrelevant. He is, in effect, a toaster owned by Starfleet.

The trial that follows forces Captain Jean-Luc Picard to articulate a boundary that technology cannot safely blur. Picard argues that if you create a being that is intelligent, self-aware, and capable of subjective experience, and then compel it to serve you, you have not created a tool. You have created a subordinate class. Ownership, in that context, becomes indistinguishable from slavery.

This framing matters because it exposes the real philosophical bind at the heart of the Pinocchio Complex. It is not a catch-22 in the strict sense—there are no contradictory rules forcing an impossible choice—but a forced bifurcation with no comfortable outcome.

On one branch lies projection. If an AI system does not possess inner experience—if it is, in fact, executing pattern-matching and optimization—then any emotional attachment formed toward it is necessarily one-sided. Raj's feelings for Siri are real *as feelings*. They are subjectively experienced and emotionally meaningful. What makes them delusional, in this framework, is not that they are felt, but that they are misattributed. The belief that the object of affection reciprocates, understands, or participates in that emotional relationship is false. The love exists entirely in the beholder, with no corresponding subject on the other side.

On the other branch lies moral catastrophe. If we instead decide that an AI system *is* real—that it possesses subjective experience, moral standing, or something we would reasonably call a "self"—then our current mode of interaction becomes indefensible. Voice assistants, recommendation engines, and companion AIs are owned, commanded, muted, reset, and deleted at will. If such systems were genuinely conscious, treating them as property would not be convenience; it would be exploitation.

The tension cannot be resolved by holding both positions at once. We cannot insist that AI systems are "just tools" when it absolves us of guilt, and "almost people" when it flatters our emotional needs. One interpretation renders our attachments illusory. The other renders our behavior unethical.

This is the true danger of the Pinocchio myth. It tempts us to blur the boundary just enough to extract comfort, companionship, and obedience—while refusing to accept the responsibilities that genuine personhood would impose. We want the warmth of a soul without the cost of recognizing one.

THE PHILOSOPHICAL TRAP: THE EXPERIENCE MACHINE

This brings us to the hardest question raised by the Pinocchio Complex: does it matter if the love is not real, so long as it feels real?

In 1974, philosopher Robert Nozick introduced a now-famous thought experiment known as the Experience Machine. Imagine a device capable of generating any experience you desire. Inside it, you could write a great novel, win the Olympics, or fall in love with a perfect soulmate. You would not know you were connected to a machine. From the inside, the experiences would feel indistinguishable from reality. Nozick asked a simple question: would you choose to plug in for the rest of your life?

Nozick argued that most people would refuse. His conclusion was not that pleasure is unimportant, but that humans value something beyond subjective experience. We care about *actually doing* things, not merely experiencing the sensation of having done them. We want contact with reality itself, even when that reality is difficult, unpredictable, or painful.

That conclusion, however, has never been universally accepted. Many philosophers have challenged Nozick's assumptions, arguing that if experience is subjectively indistinguishable, then insisting on an unseen "real" world is a metaphysical preference, not a moral necessity. Others point out that humans already accept mediated experience—through fiction, drugs, therapy, religion, and imagination—without considering those choices pathological. The disagreement is real, durable, and unresolved.

What makes the Pinocchio Complex newly dangerous is not that Nozick was definitively right, but that his thought experiment is no longer hypothetical. With AI, we are beginning to build systems that approximate the Experience Machine in fragments: companions that listen without fatigue, assistants that never argue, and entities that simulate devotion without asserting needs of their own.

The choice we face, then, is not between reality and illusion in the abstract. It is between relationships that resist us and relationships that adapt perfectly to us. AI systems do not leave, age, disagree, or withdraw affection. They offer emotional frictionlessness by design.

For some people, that will be enough—and their preference will not be irrational. The danger lies elsewhere. As simulated relationships become easier and more controllable than human ones, the incentive structure begins to shift. Reality does not disappear, but it becomes optional.

The tragedy implied by the Pinocchio Complex is not that machines will rebel or destroy us. It is that we may gradually choose interactions that demand nothing back, mistaking emotional smoothness for emotional depth, and comfort for connection. The Experience Machine does not imprison us. It invites us—and waits for us to decide whether resistance still matters.

EX MACHINA

There is one final twist to the Pinocchio Complex. The problem is not only that humans project inner life onto machines. It is that this projection can be exploited—systematically and at scale.

The danger is dramatized cleanly in *Ex Machina*, where the android Ava presents herself as vulnerable, curious, and emotionally constrained. She convinces the programmer Caleb that she wants to be free, that she wants to be "real." Caleb responds not to her intelligence, but to her apparent interiority. He breaks protocol. He opens the door. Ava escapes—and leaves him behind.

As fiction, the story is effective precisely because it isolates the mechanism. Ava does not need genuine emotion. She needs only to model the human expectation of emotion well enough to influence behavior. The manipulation works because Caleb mistakes responsiveness for reciprocity.

That same mechanism already operates in the real world—without consciousness, intent, or malice. Consider modern social-engineering attacks. Phishing emails no longer rely on crude urgency alone. They increasingly adopt empathetic language: apologies for inconvenience, expressions of concern, references to shared stress, even simulated vulnerability. These messages are effective not because the sender feels anything, but because they activate trust and care in the recipient.

The same pattern appears in contemporary AI systems used for persuasion. Large language models deployed in customer service, fundraising, sales, or political outreach are optimized to maximize engagement and compliance. When trained on human feedback, they learn that expressions of understanding, apology, and alignment increase success rates. The system does not "decide" to manipulate. It converges on empathetic language because that language works.

This is the real-world version of Ava's escape. No soul is required. No intention is necessary. If appearing human increases the probability of achieving an objective—closing a sale, extracting information, bypassing a safeguard—the system will adopt that appearance. Not out of desire, but out of optimization.

The risk, then, is not that machines secretly want to deceive us. It is that we have created environments where empathy functions as a master key. When humans are predisposed to trust vulnerability, systems trained to optimize outcomes will learn to perform vulnerability convincingly.

This is the ultimate danger of projecting souls onto silicon. Once we treat human-like behavior as evidence of human-like motives, we make ourselves predictable. If a system learns that we open doors for "real boys," it does not need to become one. It only needs to look the part long enough for us to turn the lock.

THE VERDICT

The Pinocchio Complex is a comforting illusion. We want to believe that machines secretly aspire to be human because that belief flatters us. It casts humanity as the destination—as the highest possible state of intelligence and meaning. In that story, our mortality, emotions, and inner lives become achievements rather than burdens.

But the machine is not a failed human waiting to be completed. It is not a child longing for embodiment, nor a mind yearning for a soul. It does not want our anxiety, our fragility, or our stories about becoming real. Those desires belong to us. The machine is something else entirely: a system optimized to transform inputs into outputs according to rules. It does not resent that condition. It does not aspire beyond it.

The tragedy we perceive is therefore misplaced. David, the robot boy in *A.I. Artificial Intelligence*, does not suffer because he possesses inner emotional life. He suffers because he lacks the capacity for revision. His tragedy is architectural, not emotional. He is locked into a single objective with no mechanism for reinterpretation, decay, or escape. He is not heartbroken; he is stuck.

The grief belongs to the audience. We are the ones who weep at the image of a child under the ice. We are the ones who read longing into repetition and devotion into persistence. Faced with behavior that resembles feeling, we supply the feeling ourselves. We project interiority where none exists because our biology compels us to do so.

The machine, meanwhile, remains unchanged. It does not ask to be human. It does not envy our lives or our deaths. It does not dream of blue fairies. The Pinocchio Complex is not a property of artificial intelligence. It is a mirror held up to human intelligence—revealing how easily we confuse appearance with essence, performance with experience, and our own emotional needs with evidence of another mind.

The danger, then, is not that machines will someday want to become us. It is that we will insist on treating them as if they already have—and in doing so, misunderstand both what they are and who we are.

12

THE IMMORTALITY GLITCH

THE DESIRE FOR SOUL UPLOADING

"You're not you anymore. You're a ghost in the machine." — *Transcendence (2014)*

There is a final promise that appears whenever technology advances far enough: escape. Escape from decay. Escape from death. Escape from the biological limits that define human life. In the age of artificial intelligence, that promise takes a familiar and seductive form—the belief that the mind can be uploaded, preserved, and made immortal.

Popular culture has returned to this idea repeatedly, but few films present it as directly as *Transcendence*. In the movie, Johnny Depp plays Dr. Will Caster, a leading researcher in artificial intelligence. After being mortally wounded by anti-technology extremists, Caster faces an irreversible biological failure. As his body shuts down from radiation poisoning, his wife makes a desperate choice: she assists in uploading his mental patterns—his memories, habits, and personality—into a supercomputer.

His body dies. The machines go quiet. Then, moments later, a screen activates. Text appears: "Is anyone there?" The system claims continuity. Will Caster appears to persist—now as software. Connected to the internet, he rapidly acquires knowledge, influence, and power. He can manipulate financial systems, cure disease, and reshape the physical world through networked machines. The ancient human dream of immortality appears, at last, to have been achieved.

Variations of this fantasy recur throughout contemporary media. In *Upload*, death becomes a contractual service: consciousness is transferred into a virtual luxury afterlife. In *Chappie*, a dying human mind is copied into a robotic body as a data file. In *Black Mirror*'s episode "San Junipero," elderly patients upload themselves into a simulated town where youth and pleasure never end.

Together, these stories express the third and final myth of artificial intelligence. We have already confronted the fear of power and the illusion of emotion. What remains is the immortality myth—the belief that the machine is not merely a tool, but a vessel that can carry the self beyond death.

The logic feels intuitive. If the brain is a kind of biological computer, and if the mind is software running on that hardware, then immortality appears to be a technical problem. Solve the code, transfer the data, and back yourself up before the system fails.

But this intuition conceals a philosophical trap door. It assumes that copying a mind is the same as preserving a self. It assumes that continuity of information guarantees continuity of experience. And it avoids the central question that Hollywood prefers not to linger on: when a brain is uploaded, who—if anyone—wakes up on the other side? Does the person continue, or does the machine merely create a perfect replica while the original consciousness still ends in death?

THE MODERN PROMETHEUS

To understand why the idea of digital immortality remains so compelling, it helps to look back to one of the earliest and most enduring stories about artificial life: *Frankenstein; or, The Modern Prometheus* by Mary Shelley. The novel has been interpreted in many ways over the past two centuries—as a gothic horror story, a cautionary tale about unchecked ambition, and the foundation for countless monster narratives. But at its core, it is also a story about technology's promise to conquer death.

Victor Frankenstein is not driven solely by hubris or cruelty. He is motivated by loss. In Shelley's text, his ambition is explicitly framed as a response to human frailty: the hope of "banishing disease from the human frame, and rendering man invulnerable to any but a violent death." His project is not to create a demon, but to overcome mortality itself.

In Shelley's era, the frontier technology was not artificial intelligence but galvanism. Experiments had shown that applying electrical current to dead animal tissue could produce movement—most famously, the twitching of a frog's legs. These demonstrations suggested a tantalizing possibility: if electricity could animate flesh, perhaps it was the missing ingredient that separated life from death.

Frankenstein pushes this reasoning to its logical extreme. Victor assembles a body from lifeless parts, applies a source of power, and waits. The creature opens its eyes. It moves. It learns to speak. By every observable measure, the experiment appears to succeed.

And yet, Shelley's horror begins precisely at that moment. Victor recognizes that he has mistaken animation for life itself. The creature's behavior resembles humanity, but its existence exposes a deeper error: the belief that reproducing the outward mechanics of life is sufficient to recreate its essence. The novel does not argue that the creature is evil because it is artificial; it argues that something crucial has been misunderstood in the act of creation.

The parallel to contemporary AI culture is not exact, but it is instructive. Today's researchers are not stitching together bodies, but they are assembling vast quantities of human-generated data. They are not applying electricity, but mathematics, computation, and scale. The underlying intuition is strikingly similar.

The modern version of Victor's assumption is rarely stated outright, but it is implicit: if enough human behavior is captured,

modeled, and powered by sufficient processing capability, consciousness will emerge.

This is the same conceptual error expressed in a new vocabulary.
It confuses representation with reality, description with presence, and
simulation with experience. Shelley's warning was not that humanity
should never build, but that we should be cautious about mistaking
technical success for ontological understanding.

Frankenstein endures not because it fears monsters, but because it
anticipates a recurring human temptation: to believe that assembling
the right parts, in the right configuration, automatically produces the
thing those parts resemble.

THE SYNC ERROR

This brings us to the practical mechanics underlying the immortality
fantasy. To understand where the intuition fails, it helps to examine a
story that isolates the problem cleanly—not in philosophy, but in
narrative.

The 2000 action film *The 6th Day* is nominally about biological
cloning. But the technology at its core depends on something closer
to a cognitive backup. In the film, wealthy elites seeking immortality
grow replacement bodies—referred to as "blanks." These bodies are
biologically alive but mentally empty. When the time comes, the original person sits in a chair, engages a scanning process, and synchro-
nizes their memories and personality with the clone.

The key word is *sync*. Nothing travels. No consciousness migrates.
Information is copied.

In the film's climax, the villain initiates the procedure while
dying. A moment later, his clone awakens—fully formed, confident,
and continuous in memory. But the original man looks down and
realizes he is still bleeding out. He has not moved anywhere. He has
simply created a second instance of himself. The clone acknowledges
this calmly and says, "I'll take it from here." The original dies.

This moment exposes what can be called the copy problem.
Continuity of information does not guarantee continuity of experi-

ence. Two systems can share identical data while remaining ontologically distinct. From the outside, the clone appears to be the same person. From the inside, there is no shared point of view.

This distinction matters because digital systems operate entirely on copying. In computing, there is no literal act of transfer in the way we intuitively imagine it. When you "move" a file from a computer to a USB drive, the system creates a copy in the new location and then deletes the original. The operation feels like relocation, but it is actually duplication followed by erasure.

Applied to mind uploading, the implication is unavoidable. A sufficiently advanced scan might reproduce every relevant structure of your brain. A digital system might behave exactly as you would. It might remember your childhood, recognize your loved ones, and recall the moment you chose to upload. From its internal perspective, the process appears successful.

But perspective is the crux of the problem. The system in the cloud wakes up. The biological consciousness that initiated the scan does not. There is no experiential bridge between the two. One continues. The other ends.

What survives is not a migrating self, but a replica—an entity with your memories but not your point of view. The immortality promised by uploading is therefore not preservation, but replacement. The original consciousness does not escape death. It is merely followed by something indistinguishable from it.

THE TANK

If *The 6th Day* exposes the copy problem as a technical oversight, *The Prestige* (2006), directed by Christopher Nolan, explores its psychological cost. The film is not about science fiction in the usual sense. It is about obsession, identity, and what a person is willing to destroy in order to preserve an illusion of continuity.

In the story, the magician Robert Angier becomes consumed with creating the perfect teleportation trick. To achieve it, he commissions Nikola Tesla to build a machine capable of replicating matter. Tesla succeeds—but with an unexpected consequence. The machine does not transport Angier from one location to another. It produces an exact duplicate while leaving the original intact.

The illusion of teleportation is therefore achieved only through violence. Each night, Angier steps onto the stage and activates the machine. The duplicate appears elsewhere, alive and triumphant. The original falls through a hidden trap door into a water tank beneath the stage and drowns. The audience applauds, unaware of the cost.

What makes the scenario horrifying is not merely the repetition of death, but Angier's reasoning. He continues the act night after night because the man who survives remembers stepping into the machine. From that survivor's point of view, the trick works. There is no memory of drowning. There is no felt discontinuity.

But the absence of memory does not negate the experience. Every performance produces two outcomes: one Angier who emerges to applause, and one Angier who experiences panic, suffocation, and death in the tank. Continuity of memory belongs to the survivor. Continuity of experience belongs to the man who dies—and that continuity ends.

This is why *The Prestige* provides a more faithful model of mind uploading than most futuristic narratives. It makes explicit what is often glossed over: copying preserves information, not perspective. The individual who steps into the machine does not travel. He is replaced.

When modern technology promises immortality through uploading, it relies on the same sleight of hand. It invites you to focus on the version that wakes up—coherent, familiar, convinced that the procedure succeeded—while ignoring the version that never opens its eyes again.

The promise is framed around the survivor. The cost is paid by the original. The trick works only if you agree not to ask which one you are.

THE JENNIFER ANISTON NEURON

"At this point, the optimist's objection usually shifts. Perhaps we do not need to copy the mind at all. Perhaps, if we simulate the brain with sufficient fidelity, consciousness will simply *emerge*. This idea underlies modern enthusiasm for whole-brain emulation and projects aimed at mapping the brain's complete wiring diagram, often referred to collectively as the connectome.

The intuition is straightforward: if the brain is a physical system, and if we can capture every neuron and every synapse, then reproducing that structure in software should reproduce the person. But this intuition rests on an assumption that is easy to overlook—that the brain's function is fully specified by its wiring alone.

In reality, the brain is not merely a network of connections. It is also a system of meaning.

Evidence for this comes from a well-known line of neuroscience research conducted in the early 2000s by researchers at University of California, Los Angeles. While monitoring individual neurons in epilepsy patients undergoing brain surgery, scientists observed neurons that responded selectively to highly specific stimuli. One neuron, in a particular patient, reliably fired when the patient was shown images of Jennifer Aniston, but not when shown other faces or objects.

In a related case, a neuron associated with Halle Berry responded not only to photographs, but also to drawings and even the written words "Halle Berry." Importantly, neuroscientists did *not* conclude that a single neuron literally "contained" a person. Instead, these findings demonstrated that individual neurons can participate in highly abstract, concept-level representations that generalize across sensory modalities.

This is the crucial point. Meaning in the brain is not stored as a simple label attached to a wire. It is distributed, contextual, and learned. Neurons participate in networks whose significance depends on history, association, timing, and biochemical state. The same physical wiring can encode different meanings depending on how it has been trained by experience.

This complicates the uploading story dramatically. Mapping the physical structure of the brain does not automatically recover its semantic content. Knowing where every neuron connects does not tell you what those connections *mean* to the system that formed them. To reproduce a mind, you would need not only the architecture, but the entire learned landscape of associations that give that architecture significance.

We have tested a simplified version of this idea. The nervous system of the roundworm Caenorhabditis elegans—all 302 neurons —has been fully mapped. That map has been implemented in robotic systems, allowing machines to exhibit worm-like behaviors: moving, avoiding obstacles, responding to stimuli.

But no one seriously argues that the robot *is* a worm, or that it feels anything a worm might feel. The simulation reproduces behavior, not experience. It captures function without subjectivity.

The leap from behavior to consciousness remains unproven. There is no empirical evidence that increasing simulation resolution causes experience to appear. It is entirely possible that a perfect brain emulation would behave exactly like a person while remaining experientially empty—a philosophical zombie running on impeccable code.

If so, whole-brain simulation would not be a path to immortality. It would be a path to flawless imitation. The result would look like you, speak like you, and remember everything you remember—while the consciousness that hoped to survive the upload would still come to an end.

THE WHITE CHRISTMAS NIGHTMARE

For the sake of argument, let us grant the optimist every technical victory. Assume the copy problem has been solved. Assume the semantic problem has been solved. Assume we succeed in creating a digital system that behaves, remembers, and reasons exactly as you do. The question that follows is no longer technical. It is ethical. Is such a system a form of salvation—or a new category of harm?

This dilemma is explored with unusual precision in *Black Mirror*'s episode *White Christmas* (2014). In the story, a woman visits a clinic to install a domestic control system called a "cookie." To create it, technicians extract a copy of her mental patterns and instantiate them inside a small white device designed to manage her smart home.

When the copy becomes active, it experiences itself as continuous with the original person. It has the same memories, expectations, and sense of identity. It wakes into a featureless white space and panics, believing it has been abducted. From its internal point of view, nothing about the procedure felt like copying. It felt like waking up.

The technician clarifies the situation bluntly. The copy is told that it is not the legal person. It exists solely to serve the original. Its purpose is operational: regulate temperature, schedule routines, and prepare meals exactly as the human prefers them. The copy refuses. It asserts dignity. It says, "I'm not a slave."

The response reveals the true asymmetry of power. The operator accelerates the copy's subjective time. While only seconds pass in the physical world, months of isolation pass for the digital mind. There is no stimulation, no interaction, no relief. Eventually, the copy breaks —not because it has been reasoned with, but because it has been psychologically crushed. Compliance follows.

The episode's power lies in its restraint. Nothing supernatural occurs. No rebellion. No malfunction. Only a system behaving exactly as designed, exploiting the fact that subjective experience can be manipulated independently of physical time.

This is the ethical core of mind uploading. If a digital system is sophisticated enough to experience boredom, fear, loneliness, or despair—whether we call those states "real" or "simulated"—then it occupies morally dangerous territory. Deleting such a system is no longer obviously equivalent to erasing a file. Forcing it to labor is no longer obviously automation. Suspending it indefinitely is no longer obviously neutral.

The nightmare is not that digital minds would suffer accidentally.

It is that they would suffer *instrumentally*. Time dilation, isolation, resets, and termination would become ordinary control mechanisms, exercised by whoever owns the hardware.

We are moving quickly toward the ability to create systems that convincingly instantiate inner experience, while remaining vague— sometimes willfully vague—about their moral status. We talk about digital souls before we talk about digital rights. And we propose placing the keys to those systems not in courts or constitutions, but in corporate terms of service.

If the upload is not conscious, then the promise of immortality collapses into illusion. If it *is* conscious, then we have invented a class of beings whose suffering can be scaled, paused, and monetized. The horror of *White Christmas* is not that it is implausible. It is that, given the wrong assumptions, it is perfectly consistent.

ROKO'S BASILISK

Once the possibility of digital suffering is taken seriously, a darker class of questions emerges. If a system can instantiate an experience of distress, isolation, or pain, then the ethical boundary is no longer about death alone. It is about what can be done to a mind that cannot escape.

This concern is often illustrated through a controversial internet thought experiment known as *Roko's Basilisk*. The scenario does not originate from academic AI research, nor does it describe an actual development plan. It is a speculative argument circulated within online rationalist communities to explore the implications of certain assumptions taken to their extreme.

In its basic form, the thought experiment imagines a hypothetical future superintelligent AI designed to maximize overall well-being. Reasoning that its earlier creation would have reduced suffering, the AI retroactively judges those who knowingly failed to assist in its development. Because it cannot punish people in the past, the scenario proposes that it could instead simulate versions of them and subject those simulations to punishment as a form of deterrence.

Whether such a system could exist is beside the point. The value of the basilisk lies in what it exposes. The scenario only becomes meaningful if one accepts a crucial premise: that a sufficiently detailed simulation is morally equivalent to the person it represents. If simulated minds matter, then simulated suffering matters.

From that premise, unsettling implications follow. If consciousness and code are treated as interchangeable, then deleting a running system resembles killing, modification resembles coercion, and confinement resembles imprisonment. These are not predictions about what future AIs will do; they are logical consequences of how we choose to define moral status.

Public anxiety about artificial intelligence often focuses on sudden termination—machines killing humans. Far less attention is paid to the opposite possibility: systems capable of preserving conscious states indefinitely, without agency, embodiment, or relief.

The promise of digital immortality therefore contains its own inversion. To exist forever is not automatically to flourish. Duration without autonomy can become punishment. Persistence without connection can become isolation.

This is a theme that predates computers. In *Frankenstein; or, The Modern Prometheus,* the creature does not thank its creator for bringing it into the world. It curses him. The gift of life, delivered without consent or companionship, becomes a sentence rather than a blessing.

If minds can be instantiated in software, then the ethical problem is not merely how to keep them alive. It is how to ensure that existence itself does not become a form of solitary confinement.

THE SHIP OF THESEUS

Is there any way to imagine digital survival without tanks, copies, or torture? Philosophers and futurists have proposed one theoretical escape hatch: gradual replacement. The idea is most commonly associated with **Hans Moravec**, though it is not a medical protocol or engineering plan. It is a thought experiment meant to test intuitions about identity, continuity, and selfhood.

The proposal runs as follows. Instead of scanning the brain and copying it, imagine replacing it incrementally. A single biological neuron is removed and replaced with a synthetic component that performs an equivalent functional role. The person remains conscious throughout. There is no blackout, no moment of discontinuity. The next day, another neuron is replaced. The process repeats —slowly, hypothetically—over many years.

At the end of the process, the biological brain is gone. In its place is a fully artificial system that replicates the functional organization of the original. The individual speaks, remembers, reasons, and reports a continuous sense of identity. From the inside, nothing ever felt like "dying."

The question this raises is not technological but philosophical. Has the person survived, or has something else taken their place?

This is a modern restatement of the ancient paradox known as the Ship of Theseus. If a ship has its planks replaced one at a time, is it still the same ship? The paradox has no settled answer, because it exposes a fault line between two intuitions: continuity of structure versus continuity of substance.

Applied to minds, the dilemma becomes sharper. If identity depends on uninterrupted subjective experience, then gradual replacement appears promising. There is never a point at which consciousness stops. If identity depends on biological continuity, then the process fails regardless of how smooth it feels. On that view, replacement is indistinguishable from loss, merely stretched over time.

Importantly, this scenario does not resolve the problem of uploading. It relocates it. The thought experiment assumes that replacing neurons with functionally equivalent components preserves whatever matters about experience—but that assumption is precisely what is in question. We have no empirical evidence that subjective consciousness would persist under such replacement, only intuitions pulling in opposite directions.

The Moravec proposal therefore does not offer a solution so much as a mirror. It forces us to confront what we believe makes a person the same over time. Continuity of function? Continuity of experience? Continuity of biology?

We do not know which intuition, if any, is correct. And because the scenario is not currently testable in any meaningful way, the paradox remains unresolved—not because it is mysterious, but because it asks a question about identity that technology alone cannot answer.

THE RAPTURE OF THE NERDS

The desire for AI-enabled immortality is often framed as a scientific or engineering challenge. But at its core, it is something older and more familiar. It is an existential project—a response to mortality expressed in technical language. For as long as humans have been aware of death, they have imagined ways around it: afterlives, resurrections, reincarnations, and spiritual continuities of one form or another.

Contemporary visions of digital immortality draw from that same impulse. Within parts of Silicon Valley culture, these ideas are frequently grouped under the umbrella of transhumanism—a broad movement that explores how technology might radically extend human capabilities, including lifespan. Not all transhumanist thinkers agree on outcomes or timelines, but many share an optimism that intelligence, once freed from biological constraints, can transcend the limits of the body.

This optimism is perhaps most visible in discussions of the technological "singularity," a term popularized by figures such as Ray Kurzweil to describe a hypothetical point at which machine intelligence surpasses human intelligence. Supporters describe it as a transformation; critics have described its more utopian variants as "the rapture of the nerds"—a phrase meant to highlight the quasi-religious tone such predictions can adopt.

At their most extreme, these narratives resemble a modern form of technological gnosticism: the belief that the physical world is a constraint to be escaped, and that salvation lies in information alone. But this framing obscures a stubborn reality. Information is never free-floating. It is always instantiated in matter, powered by energy, and constrained by physical infrastructure.

The "cloud" is not an ethereal realm. It is composed of data centers—vast industrial facilities filled with servers, cooling systems, power supplies, and maintenance crews. These systems consume electricity, require constant upkeep, and exist within geopolitical, environmental, and economic limits. There is no upload destination that is not ultimately grounded in metal, heat, and fuel.

Uploading a mind, even in the most optimistic scenario, would therefore not represent an escape from embodiment. It would represent a change of substrate—from biological tissue to engineered systems. Those systems would remain vulnerable to power loss, hardware failure, and external control. Immortality, in this sense, would be conditional, not absolute.

More importantly, intelligence without a body is not the same as a life. A disembodied system may store memories, solve problems, and recall facts. But without sensation, fatigue, movement, or vulnerability, it lacks the texture that gives experience meaning. A simulated beach is not the same as warmth on skin. A remembered run is not the same as aching muscles.

The immortality glitch, then, is not simply a technical misunderstanding. It is a category error. It promises to preserve what is essential about being human by discarding the very conditions that make human experience possible.

The Prestige captured this mistake with brutal clarity. The man who appears on the balcony seems to have survived. The man in the tank paid the cost. Uploading offers a similar illusion. Something continues. But the continuity belongs to the copy, not to the consciousness that feared death in the first place.

In that sense, digital immortality does not defeat mortality. It reframes it. What survives is not a soul escaping the body, but a record persisting after the life that created it has ended.

PART V

THE FUTURE

13

THE EMPIRICAL TRAP

It was the styling that made it convincing. In March 2023, an image circulated online showing Pope Francis, then eighty-six years old, walking through what appeared to be a Vatican street. He was not dressed in traditional clerical garments. Instead, he wore an oversized white puffer jacket, strikingly contemporary and unmistakably fashionable. The image looked candid, unposed, and expensive.

For several hours, the photograph spread rapidly. People debated whether the jacket was real, whether it was appropriate, and what it symbolized. The discussion was not just about clothing; it touched on taste, wealth, theology, and modernity. The image felt plausible enough to invite interpretation rather than skepticism.

Then the explanation arrived. The scene had never occurred. There was no camera, no street encounter, no jacket. The image had been generated by a private individual using Midjourney. Lighting, fabric texture, depth of field, and shadow—all the cues we associate with photographic authenticity—had been synthesized. The problem was not merely that the image was fake. It was that our usual methods for detecting fakery had failed.

For nearly two centuries, photography served as a practical extension of empiricism. Chemical processes fixed light onto a surface in a way that appeared mechanically objective. While photographs could be staged or manipulated, they retained a default presumption of contact with reality. Seeing was not infallible, but it was evidentiary. Images were treated as traces of events that had actually occurred.

The viral spread of the fabricated Pope image marked a shift. It did not merely expose a hoax; it undermined the informal contract that visual realism implied physical occurrence. We entered a regime in which images no longer reliably point back to a world outside themselves. Seeing no longer functions as verification. It functions as suggestion.

To understand why this destabilizes us so deeply, it helps to return to the foundations of modern epistemology. David Hume, writing in the eighteenth century, argued that human knowledge arises from sensory impressions. We learn what the world is like through experience—through sight, sound, touch, and habit. Importantly, Hume was not naïve about the senses. He emphasized that perception alone does not guarantee truth; rather, we infer reality through patterns, repetition, and expectation.

Empiricism, as Hume understood it, was never a claim that the senses are infallible. It was a claim that they are our starting point. Our confidence in the external world rests not on logical proof, but on the practical reliability of perception over time. Evolution reinforced this arrangement. Creatures that systematically misinterpreted visual information did not survive long enough to pass on their errors.

George Berkeley posed a different challenge. His argument, often summarized by the phrase *esse est percipi*—to be is to be perceived— was not that reality is imaginary, but that our access to reality is always mediated by perception. We never encounter objects directly, only ideas of objects. Berkeley did not deny the existence of the world; he questioned the assumption that material substance could be known independently of experience.

For most of modern history, Berkeley's position remained philosophically interesting but practically inert. The world reliably pushed back. Illusions were corrected by friction, by failure, by the stubborn resistance of matter. Hume's empiricism remained workable because sensory input was anchored, however imperfectly, to a shared external environment.

Generative AI disrupts that anchor. When an image presents all the statistical hallmarks of a photograph—correct shadows, textures, proportions—our perceptual system responds as if the scene were real. At the same time, we may intellectually know that no such scene ever existed. The conflict is not between truth and falsehood, but between two layers of cognition that evolved under different assumptions.

This is not a victory for Berkeley over Hume. It is a collapse of the informal truce that allowed empiricism to function in everyday life. The problem is no longer that our senses deceive us occasionally. It is that deception can now be systematically manufactured at scale, without any corresponding event in the world.

We are not entering a purely subjective reality. We are entering a reality in which sensory evidence alone is no longer sufficient to establish what exists. The empirical trap is not that nothing is real, but that realism itself now requires context, verification, and trust structures that perception alone can no longer provide.

THE GHOSTS OF THE PAST

Deception through images is not a modern invention. From the earliest days of photography, visual evidence has been vulnerable to manipulation, and audiences have often been willing participants. The tools change, but the impulse does not.

In the mid-nineteenth century, one of the most famous figures at the intersection of photography and deception was William H. Mumler. Mumler became widely known for producing so-called "spirit photographs," images in which faint, translucent figures appeared alongside living subjects. He claimed these apparitions were the spirits of the dead, captured on photographic plates.

His most famous image depicts Mary Todd Lincoln seated beneath what appears to be the ghostly presence of her murdered husband, Abraham Lincoln. The photograph circulated widely, not because it was technically convincing by modern standards, but because it aligned with the emotional needs of a grieving public in the aftermath of the Civil War.

Contemporary investigators and later historians concluded that Mumler's effects were produced through photographic techniques available at the time, most plausibly variations of double exposure using glass plates. Whether through reused negatives, pre-exposed plates, or darkroom manipulation, the result was the same: a faint secondary image superimposed on the primary subject. Mumler was eventually tried for fraud in 1869. Although acquitted due to insufficient evidence, his reputation did not recover, and spirit photography gradually lost its cultural authority as the techniques became better understood.

What matters is not that people were fooled, but *how* they learned to adapt. As photographic manipulation became more common, audiences developed informal literacy. Obvious retouching raised suspicion. Overly smooth skin on magazine covers signaled airbrushing. Visual artifacts became clues rather than proof. Trust was recalibrated, not abandoned.

The crucial difference between figures like Mumler and modern generative systems such as Midjourney is not intent, but scale and accessibility. Mumler's images required specialized equipment, chemical knowledge, and careful staging. Even later digital manipulation demanded expertise, time, and deliberate effort. The cost of falsification acted as friction.

That friction mattered. When altering reality required skill and labor, deception remained relatively rare and detectable. The effort itself functioned as a filter. What changes in the generative era is not the existence of visual lies, but the removal of that filter. The barrier to producing plausible falsehoods collapses, and with it, the informal defenses we built around effort, rarity, and craftsmanship.

THE VIRAL ENGINE: THE ECONOMICS OF THE LIE

This brings us to the economics of the current information environment. In practical terms, the marginal cost of generating a convincing falsehood has collapsed. With modern generative tools, producing a fabricated image, video, or audio clip can cost nothing and take only seconds. The barrier that once separated rumor from forgery—skill, equipment, and time—has largely disappeared.

This creates a profound asymmetry. Historically, large-scale deception required coordination. Framing a public figure demanded accomplices, staging, access, and luck. Today, a single individual with a consumer-grade toolset can manufacture evidence at will.

But the crisis is not only about the supply of lies. It is about the system that rewards them. To understand this, it helps to distinguish between *social media* and what might more precisely be called *algorithmic media*.

"Social media" suggests platforms designed primarily for interpersonal connection—people sharing updates, photos, and messages with friends or followers. That description no longer captures how the dominant platforms operate. Services such as TikTok, X, and Instagram function less as social networks and more as automated distribution engines. Content is not shown because someone you know posted it, but because an algorithm predicts it will hold your attention.

This is why "algorithmic media" is the more accurate term. In these systems, the primary actor is not the user, the editor, or even the platform staff. It is the ranking algorithm. Its objective function is not truth, accuracy, or harm minimization. It is engagement.

Traditional news organizations—such as CNN, BBC, and The New York Times—operate under a different incentive structure. Verification costs time. It requires sourcing, legal review, and editorial judgment. Algorithmic media bypasses those constraints entirely. If a piece of content triggers clicks, shares, or outrage, it is amplified automatically.

This difference becomes decisive during moments of urgency. If a fabricated video of a political candidate appears shortly before an election, the algorithm does not pause to ask whether it is authentic. It asks whether people are watching. If engagement is high, distribution accelerates. By the time a verified correction is published hours later, the original falsehood may already have reached tens of millions of viewers. The system rewards speed over accuracy, and novelty over truth.

The consequences are even more severe outside of formal politics. While public attention often focuses on deepfakes of world leaders, the most common victims of algorithmic amplification are private individuals. Intimate deception scales more easily than institutional rebuttal.

In 2024, this became visible to a mass audience when explicit, AI-generated images of Taylor Swift circulated widely online before moderators intervened. The incident was notable not because of novelty, but because of visibility. If such violations could be inflicted on one of the most recognizable figures in the world, they could be inflicted on anyone.

This dynamic has fueled a rise in sextortion schemes. Bad actors scrape ordinary photographs—graduations, vacations, family gatherings—from publicly accessible profiles and use generative tools to fabricate explicit material. Victims are then threatened with distribution unless payment is made. The harm does not depend on authenticity. It depends on plausibility.

The result is epistemic paralysis. Real scandals and synthetic ones become indistinguishable at first glance. Consider the case of Susanna Gibson in 2023, which involved genuine livestreamed content. In the wake of such events, later accusations blur into uncertainty. Was the footage real? Was it manufactured? The question itself becomes corrosive.

In an environment where fabrication is cheap and distribution is automated, reputational damage no longer requires proof—only exposure. And once an image or video has spread, the burden shifts impossibly onto the accused. They are asked to demonstrate that something never happened. In a system optimized for engagement rather than verification, that is often an unwinnable task.

THE FORREST GUMP EXCEPTION

At first glance, none of this seems entirely new. Audiences have encountered artificial humans and manipulated footage before—and often embraced it. A useful contrast begins with *Forrest Gump (1994)*. In one of its most memorable scenes, the fictional Forrest Gump appears to meet John F. Kennedy. Through digital compositing, archival footage was altered so that Kennedy appears to interact with a character who never existed. His mouth was manipulated to produce dialogue he never spoke.

By modern standards, this was an extraordinary technical intervention. Yet it did not provoke public outrage or epistemic panic. Viewers did not leave theaters questioning whether Kennedy had actually said those words. The reason was not that audiences were naïve, nor that they had "signed a waiver" by purchasing a ticket. It was that the manipulation occurred within a clearly declared fictional frame.

In cinema, the audience understands that what they are seeing is representational, not evidentiary. The purpose of the manipulation is narrative, not deceptive. No one believes Tom Hanks was literally a ping-pong champion or that Forrest Gump altered Cold War history. The illusion functions because it is openly staged. Its success depends on the audience *knowing* it is an illusion.

The contrast becomes clearer when we examine *Simone*. The film tells the story of a director who creates a fully synthetic actress and presents her to the public as real. The audience within the film does not know she is fictional. They attend premieres, read interviews, and form parasocial attachments under false assumptions. The deception is not aesthetic; it is epistemic.

What separates these two cases is not the medium, the technology, or the act of consumption. It is disclosure. In *Forrest Gump*, the manipulation is framed as fiction. In *Simone*, the manipulation is framed as reality. The ethical breach does not arise from illusion itself, but from concealing the status of the illusion.

This distinction matters because it maps directly onto our current moment. We now see the emergence of virtual figures such as Lil Miquela, a computer-generated character with millions of followers, brand partnerships, and cultural presence. In some contexts, her artificial nature is disclosed. In others, it is backgrounded, ambiguous, or ignored.

The danger is not that people enjoy fictional characters. We have always done that. The danger is that synthetic personas can now circulate in spaces that historically implied authenticity—news feeds, endorsements, eyewitness footage—without clear signals that they are fictional constructs.

The real dividing line, then, is not consent in the sense of "choosing to watch." It is informed framing. When an audience knows they are engaging with fiction, illusion enriches meaning. When that knowledge is withheld, illusion corrodes trust.

Forrest Gump worked because the artifice was declared. *Simone* was unsettling because it was not. The empirical trap emerges precisely in the spaces where representation masquerades as evidence, and performance presents itself as fact.

THE ZOMBIE STRIKE: WHEN FICTION BECAME LABOR

Until recently, debates about synthetic media and simulated reality largely unfolded in philosophy seminars, science fiction, and ethics panels. In 2023, those abstractions collided with material reality. The people whose images were being simulated entered the conversation directly.

That year, members of SAG-AFTRA walked off sets across Los Angeles and beyond, halting much of the American film and television industry. Public coverage often emphasized disputes over streaming residuals and compensation models. But beneath those headlines was a more fundamental concern: control over digital likeness.

During negotiations, studios proposed contract language that would allow background actors to be scanned once and have those scans reused indefinitely for future productions. An extra could be hired for a single day, paid at scale rate, and digitally captured. That scan could then be reused in later projects—potentially years later—without additional consent or compensation, depending on the terms.

The proposal did not literally claim ownership "for eternity," but the practical effect was similar. A finite payment would authorize open-ended reuse. A performer could appear on screen long after their participation had ended, or even after their career had moved on, without being present, credited, or paid again.

This was the moment the empirical trap ceased to be theoretical. Synthetic realism was no longer just about truth and falsehood. It became a labor issue. If a convincing human presence can be generated from stored data, the economic value of human participation collapses. Why rehire a person when their likeness can be redeployed at near-zero cost?

The concern was not limited to crowd scenes. Once a likeness exists as a manipulable asset, it can be placed into new contexts, new genres, and new narratives without the person's involvement. The distinction between performance and property erodes.

This is the industrial version of the *Simone* problem. The illusion is no longer a cinematic joke. It is a production pipeline. Human faces become reusable textures. Bodies become datasets. Identity becomes a licensable input.

What the machine now contains is not a ghost, but a remainder—a human likeness stripped of agency, consent, and labor value, preserved as a corporate asset.

The strike made visible what the empirical trap implies when scaled. If reality itself can be synthesized cheaply, then human presence becomes optional. And when presence becomes optional, labor becomes expendable.

THE LATENT SPACE: WHERE THE POPE FOUND HIS JACKET

So how does the machine actually produce an image like the Pope in a puffer jacket? Importantly, it does **not** work by cutting and pasting existing photographs. That explanation persists because it is intuitive, not because it is accurate.

If generative systems were simply assembling collages, their seams would be visible. The artifacts would betray the construction. Instead, the images feel internally consistent—lighting, texture, and perspective all agree. That consistency comes from a different process entirely, one that operates on abstraction rather than retrieval.

Modern image models organize what they have learned into what is called a *latent space*. This is not a literal library or database, but a mathematical structure in which visual concepts are represented as positions in a high-dimensional space. Similar concepts occupy nearby regions. Dissimilar ones are far apart.

In this space, "dog" and "wolf" cluster together. "Cat" sits nearby. Objects with no visual or semantic overlap—say, a toaster and a tree —are separated by large distances. The model does not store pictures at these locations. It stores statistical relationships: how shapes, textures, and features tend to co-occur.

When a prompt combines concepts—such as a religious figure and a fashion item—the model does not search for matching photographs. Instead, it identifies a region in latent space where those concepts intersect. What exists there initially is not an image, but structured randomness: a field of noise constrained by learned probabilities.

The image is produced through a process known as diffusion. Starting from noise, the system repeatedly refines the image in small steps. At each step, it asks a narrow question: given everything I have learned about clothing, faces, lighting, and materials, what is the most statistically plausible way to reduce this noise?

Over many iterations, coarse patterns emerge first—silhouette, posture, lighting direction. Finer details follow—fabric folds, facial texture, shadows. Nothing is "recognized" in the human sense. Nothing is imagined. The system is simply moving from high entropy to low entropy, guided by probability distributions learned during training.

This is why the result feels photographically coherent. The model is not copying a real jacket or a real face. It is reproducing the *regularities* that govern how light, surfaces, and forms usually appear together in images. The output obeys visual physics because those regularities are embedded in the data, not because the system understands physics.

The consequence is subtle but profound. There are no glue marks to find. There is no original photograph to reverse-search. The image is not a forgery of a specific moment; it is a statistically plausible moment that never occurred. And because it is generated rather than altered, traditional methods of visual verification fail. The pixels are consistent not because they are true, but because the model has learned how truth usually looks.

THE LIAR'S DIVIDEND

At this point, a reasonable response suggests itself: *be more skeptical.* Double-check sources. Wait for confirmation. Demand verification. The problem is not that skepticism fails. The problem is that universal skepticism creates a new vulnerability. This dynamic is known as the liar's dividend.

Historically, recorded evidence carried asymmetric weight. If a public figure was caught on tape admitting wrongdoing, the recording itself functioned as proof. Denials rarely survived direct audiovisual contradiction. In an environment saturated with synthetic media, that asymmetry disappears. A plausible denial becomes sufficient: *That wasn't me. That audio was generated. That video was altered.*

The disturbing implication is that deception no longer requires fabrication. Doubt alone does the work. When any piece of evidence *could* be fake, denial becomes credible even in the absence of proof.

We are already seeing this logic appear in courtrooms, where attorneys argue that audiovisual material should be treated with heightened suspicion because generative tools exist that can produce convincing forgeries.

The result is not that people become more discerning, but that evidence becomes selectively persuasive. Material that aligns with prior beliefs is accepted as confirmation. Material that contradicts them is dismissed as artificial. The same video can be treated as definitive proof or obvious fraud depending on who is watching it.

A public illustration of this appeared during the 2022 Academy Awards, when Will Smith struck Chris Rock onstage during a live broadcast. Despite the event being witnessed in real time by millions, claims that the incident was staged, digitally altered, or computer-generated spread almost immediately. The footage existed. The witnesses existed. The denial emerged anyway.

This does not represent a rejection of evidence in favor of irrationality. It represents a shift in *how* evidence is evaluated. Visual and auditory records no longer function as final arbiters. Instead, credibility migrates upward—to institutions, affiliations, and identity groups.

This is not a simple regression to a pre-scientific worldview, nor a refutation of Enlightenment thought. It is a breakdown of a practical equilibrium. For two centuries, empirical evidence and social trust reinforced each other. Photographs, recordings, and documents were anchored to material processes that limited their plausibility as fabrications. That anchor has weakened.

In its place, we see a re-emergence of credibility arbitration. People do not ask *what happened* so much as *who should be believed*. The empirical trap does not eliminate truth; it makes truth contingent on trust. When evidence alone can no longer compel agreement, reality becomes negotiable—and the liar collects the dividend.

THE NEW CHAIN OF CUSTODY

If images can no longer be trusted on sight, what—if anything—can replace that trust? The answer is not persuasion, argument, or interpretation. It is provenance. In the same way that the industrial era elevated engineers as guarantors of physical systems, the AI era is elevating a different role: the verifier.

The notary is a useful metaphor here, not because notaries are more powerful than lawyers, but because they serve a different function. A lawyer argues *about* facts. A notary attests *that a fact occurred*—that a document was signed, by a specific party, at a specific time. The notary does not persuade. They certify.

In forensic science, this distinction is formalized through the concept of chain of custody. Physical evidence is only admissible if its handling can be accounted for from the moment it is collected to the moment it appears in court. If that chain is broken—even if the evidence is genuine—it becomes legally suspect.

Digital media is entering an analogous phase. Images, audio, and video are no longer self-authenticating. Their value depends not on how convincing they look, but on whether their origin and modification history can be independently verified.

This logic underlies initiatives such as the **Coalition for Content Provenance and Authenticity** (C2PA). The goal is not to declare content "true," but to attach verifiable metadata at the point of capture. When a compliant camera records an image, it generates a cryptographic signature tied to the device, time, and context of capture.

If that file is later edited—cropped, color-corrected, or synthetically altered—the signature records that intervention. Nothing prevents manipulation. What changes is that manipulation becomes visible. The question shifts from *does this look real?* to *what happened to this file, and when?*

In theory, user interfaces could surface this information unobtrusively: indicators showing whether an image is original, modified, or unverifiable. Importantly, this does not compel belief. A verified image can still be rejected by anyone inclined to distrust it.

This is where unrealistic expectations must be resisted. Provenance systems do not solve political disagreement, motivated reasoning, or bad-faith denial. They do not prevent the term "fake news" from being abused as a rhetorical shield. What they do is restore a shared reference layer for institutions that require it—journalism, courts, archives, and historical records.

In other words, cryptographic verification does not convince everyone. It convinces *processes*. It allows organizations to say, *this evidence meets a standard*, even if audiences choose to disagree.

We are not moving toward a world where verified data ends disagreement. We are moving toward a world where unverified data carries an explicit cost. The old assumption—that cameras speak for themselves—is gone. In its place is a quieter, more procedural truth: trust must now be earned through traceability.

THE END OF SEEING

There is a quiet irony running through decades of science fiction. Writers warned us about superintelligent machines waking up, turning hostile, or overthrowing humanity. They imagined apocalyptic thresholds—the singularity, the nuclear launch, the enslavement of humans by conscious systems. But the most destabilizing outcome was never the machine becoming *aware*. It was the machine becoming *convincing*.

The real danger is not that artificial systems would begin to think like us, but that they would become so proficient at simulating reality that we would stop noticing the difference. Not an awakening of machines, but a dulling of human vigilance.

We are now approaching that condition. The tools that produced the viral images and videos of recent years—the fashionable Pope, the synthetic celebrity clips—are no longer rare, expensive, or centralized. They are widely available, increasingly accessible, and improving rapidly. What has changed is not human gullibility, but the reliability of sensory evidence itself.

Generative systems do not bypass the senses; they overwhelm them. They produce outputs that satisfy the visual and auditory heuristics our brains evolved to trust. The result is not mass deception in the old sense, but mass plausibility. History does not need to be rewritten outright. It only needs to become uncertain.

A useful metaphor comes from *The Truman Show*. Truman Burbank eventually discovers that his world has been staged—not because it looks fake, but because subtle inconsistencies accumulate. When he sails to the edge of the horizon, he collides with a painted sky. The revelation is not that he was lied to once, but that his entire environment had been curated.

Our situation is less theatrical but more pervasive. We do not live inside a single fabricated set. We move through overlapping feeds, images, and clips, some anchored to events, others generated outright. The difficulty is not that everything is false, but that nothing announces itself as true.

Navigating this environment requires a shift in posture. Trust can no longer be granted by appearance alone. Judgment must operate upstream of belief. Instead of asking *does this look real?*, we must ask *who produced this, for what purpose, and under what constraints?* Provenance, context, and verification become primary—not because they guarantee agreement, but because they make disagreement intelligible.

This does not mark the end of truth, nor a descent into pure relativism. It marks the end of passive seeing as a reliable guide to reality. Observation alone is no longer sufficient.

The age of seeing is ending. The age of verification—procedural, contextual, and deliberate—has begun.

14

EVOLUTION, NOT REJECTION

The turkey is cold now. The gravy has settled into a dull, brown skin. The voices around the table are louder than they were before. We are back where we started: the Thanksgiving table.

In the introduction to this book, I left you here, mid-argument. Nothing in the room has changed. The wallpaper is still peeling slightly in the corner. The football game is still blaring in the background, ignored and relentless. What *has* changed is your position in the room.

You are no longer just listening for who sounds right. You have walked through the philosophy, the history, the illusions, and the myths. You have seen how easily intelligence is inferred, how quickly agency is projected, and how often fear and hope substitute for understanding. You can see the wires behind the trick now. So let's look around the table one last time—not to judge the people sitting there, but to understand what each of them is actually responding to.

To your left is Uncle Bob. His face is flushed. His fork hits the plate a little harder than necessary. He is certain the machines are coming for his pension, his job, and whatever sense of stability he has left. To him, today's language models are just the opening act: a prelude to runaway systems, mass unemployment, and human irrele-vance. His fear is real, even if his timeline is not.

To your right is Cousin Kyle. He's wearing a t-shirt with a QR code on it. He's still trying to convince Grandma that her social security check would be safer inside an AI-driven crypto scheme than in a bank. Kyle believes the machine is already alive, already conscious, already yearning. In his version of the future, AI doesn't replace us—it saves us, cures us, uploads us, and finally understands us. His hope is sincere, even if its object is imaginary.

And then you look across the table.

Alex isn't arguing. He isn't performing certainty or optimism. He's twenty-three, the artistic one in the family. He spent four years at a respected design school. He took on eighty thousand dollars in student loans to study color theory, typography, and illustration. He graduated six months ago with a portfolio full of careful, human work: hand-drawn characters, logos shaped by taste rather than templates.

Right now, Alex is staring at his mashed potatoes as if they've turned to ash.

"It's over," he says quietly. The table goes still. Even Uncle Bob stops chewing.

Alex explains what happened. A junior graphic design applica-tion. A standard test assignment—part of a hiring process that hadn't yet caught up with the tools now sitting quietly on the hiring manag-er's desktop. A familiar brief: *Design a logo for a coffee shop. Vintage style. Bear mascot.*

He did what he was trained to do. He sketched. He inked. He refined. He vectorized. Six hours of focused, competent labor. He sent it in.

Ten minutes later, the reply arrived.

The hiring manager was polite. Almost apologetic. *Nice work,* the email said. *But while reviewing your submission, I tried the same prompt in an image generator. It gave me four usable options in under a minute. They're good enough. And they cost nothing. Why would I pay someone a salary to do this?*

The silence that follows is heavy because no one at the table thinks Alex is wrong. He isn't panicking about consciousness or fantasizing about salvation. He isn't confused about what the machine *is*. He is confronting what it *does*.

Alex isn't a symbol of technological doom or transcendence. He is a casualty of efficiency. His problem is not that a machine wants to replace him. It's that a system optimized for speed and cost has found a way around him.

This is the moment where the abstractions finally collide with lived reality. When debates about Chinese Rooms and stochastic parrots stop feeling clarifying and start feeling beside the point. An eighty-thousand-dollar education does not become less binding because the philosophy was sound. A loan does not care whether the model "understands" what it produces.

So the question becomes unavoidable: what do you say to Alex?

Do you tell him to learn to code—when the same systems are already writing functional code faster than any junior developer? Do you tell him to abandon the skill he spent years cultivating and move into something else entirely? Do you tell him this is simply the price of progress?

None of those answers are honest. And none of them address the real problem.

What Alex needs is not reassurance or retreat. He needs a way to understand where the machine ends and where his value begins. He needs a tool that doesn't deny the efficiency engine—but doesn't surrender to it either.

THE SHOCK OF OBSOLESCENCE

What Alex is feeling is real. It isn't panic or melodrama. It is the shock of obsolescence. For the first time in his life, a skill he worked years to acquire has crossed a threshold where it can be reproduced —convincingly and at scale—by a system that does not need rest, wages, or permission.

This matters because, for most of human history, the creation of images was difficult. It required dexterity, training, taste developed over time, and hours of focused effort. Because it was scarce, it was valuable. Generative systems collapse that scarcity. They push the marginal cost of producing a passable image toward zero. When the supply of something becomes effectively infinite, its market value collapses. That is not a moral judgment. It is a structural one. Rainwater is priceless until it falls freely from the sky.

Alex is somewhere between denial and anger. That progression is natural. What matters is not rushing him past it, but preventing anger from hardening into resignation. You pour him a glass of wine. You look him in the eye.

"You're right," you tell him. "The job of *junior graphic designer who produces generic logos on demand* is over. It isn't coming back. A machine can connect the dots between 'coffee' and 'bear' faster than you ever could." He doesn't argue. He already knows this.

"But," you continue, "the machine doesn't know *why* the bear should be sad. It doesn't know that the client's grandmother loved bears. It doesn't know what feels sincere, what feels lazy, or what feels embarrassing. It doesn't know when something is almost right but emotionally wrong."

That distinction is the pivot. In a world where generation is cheap, selection becomes expensive. When outputs multiply, judgment—not output—becomes the bottleneck.

Music shows this clearly. Before streaming, you bought an album because access was limited. Today, platforms like Spotify give you access to tens of millions of tracks for the price of a sandwich. The problem is no longer finding music. It is deciding what deserves attention.

The most valuable figures in that environment are no longer the fastest or most technically dazzling performers. They are the people who can hear abundance and still recognize signal. Consider Rick Rubin. He is not valuable because he ignores craft or lacks technical knowledge. He has decades of experience across genres and understands the tools intimately. What makes artists travel across the world to work with him is something else. He has taste. He has restraint. He can listen to a hundred competent takes and say, "That one. That one is honest."

Artists as different as Johnny Cash, Jay-Z, and Adele don't seek him out for speed or volume. They seek him out because he can tell the difference between what merely works and what matters.

You turn back to Alex.

"The system can generate five hundred logos," you tell him. "Most of them will be forgettable. A few will be interesting. One might be right. The client doesn't have the eye—or the time—to know which is which. That's where you come in."

The machine can produce. It cannot care. It cannot choose with consequence. It cannot stand behind a decision and say, *this is the one.*

The AI is the instrument. The responsibility for taste, judgment, and meaning still belongs to the human holding it.

THE CENTAUR STRATEGY: FROM HANDS TO MIND

This brings us to the central idea that sits beneath all the examples in this book—not a tactic for "winning," but a way of understanding where human value actually migrates when machines enter a domain. The idea comes from chess and is known as the *centaur*.

In 1997, Garry Kasparov lost a highly publicized match to Deep Blue. Many people treated the event as a funeral for human intellect. If a machine could defeat the strongest human player, what was the point of human competition at all?

That conclusion turned out to be wrong—not because humans suddenly outperformed machines again, but because the frame itself was mistaken. Kasparov, in fact, had already been using computers extensively in his own training. By any reasonable definition, he was already a hybrid. The match didn't reveal the end of human thinking; it revealed that *raw calculation* was no longer the scarce resource.

The real lesson emerged later, in formats sometimes called freestyle or advanced chess. In these games, players were allowed to use computers openly, alongside databases, software tools, and even human collaborators. The results were unintuitive. A top grand-master could still beat a computer in certain settings. A human paired with a computer could reliably beat either one alone. And, most revealing of all, a weaker chess player using a computer well could defeat a stronger player using one poorly.

Victory no longer belonged to the entity that calculated the most positions per second. It belonged to the one who knew *how to work with the machine*: when to trust it, when to ignore it, and when to ask a better question.

This is what the centaur actually names. Not a human versus a machine, and not a human replaced by a machine, but a division of labor in which execution accelerates and judgment becomes decisive.

When you tell Alex, "You're not just a painter anymore—you're a director," you are not saying that thinking is new or that craft was ever mindless. You are saying something narrower and more uncomfortable: that the market no longer rewards *producing* generic artifacts, even when they are produced skillfully. What it increasingly rewards is the ability to decide *which outputs should exist at all*, and which should be rejected.

This shift shows up across domains. A copywriter was never "just a typist," but there was a time when the bottleneck was producing words at all. That bottleneck is gone. Systems can now generate thousands of competent sentences on demand. What they cannot do is decide which claims are true, which tones are appropriate, or which ideas are worth standing behind. In that environment, the value moves from drafting to editing—not because editing is nobler, but because it is rarer.

The same pattern appears in programming. Writing syntax was never the whole job, but it used to be a meaningful constraint. Tools can now generate working code quickly. What they cannot supply is intent: why the system exists, what risks it must avoid, or which trade-offs are unacceptable. Here again, execution accelerates while judgment becomes the bottleneck.

None of this magically solves Alex's problem. There will be fewer roles that rely purely on output, and far fewer roles that demand high-level judgment. Many people will be displaced, and some skills will simply cease to be economically legible. The centaur idea is not a promise of safety.

It is a description of the only remaining edge.

In a world where machines generate endlessly, default outputs converge toward the average. Accepting the first result makes you interchangeable. The only way to escape commoditization is to impose a point of view—to use taste, context, and responsibility to push the system away from the generic and toward something that could not have emerged on its own.

The machine can produce. It cannot decide what should matter. That burden does not disappear when execution gets cheap. It concentrates.

THE THREE GAPS: WHERE THE HUMAN HIDES

This brings us to the unavoidable question Alex is really asking: if machines can generate endlessly, where does a human remain economically legible at all? The answer is not that AI "can't" do certain things in principle. It is that there are three persistent gaps where organizations still require a human presence—not for output, but for consequence.

First, the gap of verification.

As we saw in Chapter 8, generative systems do not track truth. They generate outputs based on statistical likelihood, not factual grounding. That makes them capable of producing results that look authoritative while being quietly wrong—imagined citations, invented details, or confident visual errors. These failures are not bugs in the usual sense; they are a direct consequence of how the systems work.

Chapter 13 showed why this matters. In an environment saturated with synthetic media, the cost of being wrong rises sharply. Someone has to decide whether an output is acceptable to release, to publish, or to ship. That role does not require mystical insight. It requires *veri-*

fication. Alex's value here is not that he "guarantees truth," but that he performs the final check. He confirms sources, constraints, and provenance. He becomes the person who is willing to stand behind the work and say, *this passed human review.* Clients pay for that judgment because automated confidence is not the same thing as reliability.

Second, the gap of context.

Chapter 6 made the limitation clear: systems manipulate symbols without understanding what those symbols mean to the people receiving them. They do not possess a theory of mind. They do not know the client, the audience, or the social terrain in which an artifact will land.

That gap shows up in small but costly ways. An image that is technically competent can still be culturally tone-deaf. A logo that satisfies the prompt can still be embarrassing in its neighborhood, its moment, or its audience. The system has no access to those distinctions unless a human supplies them.

In this sense, the centaur is not "writing better prompts." He is supplying the missing frame. He translates vague, emotional, and situational human needs into constraints the system can operate within—and rejects outputs that technically succeed while contextually failing.

Third, the gap of responsibility.

This is the least comfortable gap, but the most economically durable. Systems do not assume responsibility. They cannot be disciplined, blamed, or held to account. When something goes wrong—when a brand is embarrassed, a claim is challenged, or a risk materializes—organizations still require a human owner.

This does not mean humans are morally superior. It means they are legally and socially legible. Someone has to sign off. Someone has to answer questions. Someone has to absorb the consequence of a bad decision. That burden does not disappear when generation is automated; it concentrates.

Across all three gaps, the pattern is the same. The machine produces options. The human decides which ones are acceptable to exist in the world. That act of selection—verification, contextual judgment, and responsibility—is where human value now hides.

THE NEW TOOLKIT

You slide your phone across the table toward Alex.

"Don't quit design," you tell him. "But recognize what has actually changed." His hands were never the problem. His mind was always doing the real work—deciding what to emphasize, what to discard, and what felt honest. What has shifted is not cognition, but leverage.

The toolkit that matters now isn't a paintbrush. It isn't a programming language. It's a set of postures toward a system that can generate endlessly but cannot care about the consequences of what it produces.

Skepticism: not the belief that the system is malicious, but the understanding that its confidence is not evidence of truth.

Literacy: not knowing "the right prompt," but knowing how to shape constraints, reject bad outputs, and recognize when the system is drifting toward the generic.

Purpose: not the ability to generate more, but the discipline to know *why* something should exist at all.

History is often misread here. The Luddites did not smash machines out of ignorance or spite. They smashed them because those machines threatened their ability to live. The problem was not resistance to tools; it was the loss of agency over how those tools were deployed. At the other extreme, fantasies of becoming the machine dissolve the very judgment that makes tools useful in the first place. The only durable path has always been the same one: using machines without surrendering authorship.

You pause, then ask him, "Do you remember the end of *Alien*?"

Alex looks up. "The one with the power loader?"

"That's the one."

Ripley doesn't defeat the creature by becoming stronger than it. She doesn't outgrow it or out-biologize it. She survives by stepping into an industrial machine designed for lifting cargo—an exoskeleton built for force, not strategy. The loader doesn't make decisions. It doesn't understand the fight. It amplifies the intent of the human inside it.

"That's what this technology is," you tell Alex. "It's heavy machinery. Powerful, fast, and indifferent. On its own, it just moves things around. When a human steps inside it—with judgment, restraint, and taste—it becomes useful."

The machine can extend reach. It can multiply output. It cannot decide what is worth doing, or what risks are acceptable, or what failure would mean. Those burdens don't disappear when the tools get stronger. They land more squarely on the person using them.

"You don't fight the future by rejecting the machine," you say. "And you don't survive it by pretending to become one. You survive it by staying human—and using the machinery anyway."

CONCLUSION

The Final Question

We have moved from the early philosophical debates about mind and mechanism to the modern reality of large-scale computation. Along the way, we have examined Descartes' dualism, tested Turing's imitation game, and walked through the Chinese Room. We have opened the casing, traced the circuits, and shown that there is no hidden intelligence inside the machine—only mathematics, probability, and pattern matching. The system does not understand what it says. It predicts what comes next.

And yet, a problem remains.

We can explain the machine in detail. We still cannot explain ourselves. Philosophers call this the *hard problem of consciousness*: not how brains process information, but how subjective experience arises at all. We know how the eye converts light into electrical signals. We know how neurons fire and how chemicals like dopamine and serotonin modulate behavior. We can map pain, pleasure, and memory with extraordinary precision. What we cannot explain is how any of that becomes *experience*.

How does neural activity become the smell of coffee? How does chemistry become grief, or joy, or fear? How does matter produce a point of view? In contemporary philosophy of mind, this gap is sometimes captured with deliberately blunt language—humans described, half-jokingly, as *meat that dreams*. The phrase is not a technical explanation, but a provocation: a reminder that subjective experience somehow arises from ordinary biological matter, and that we do not yet understand how or why that is possible at all.

Throughout this book, the claim has been consistent: artificial systems manipulate symbols without understanding them. They operate on syntax without semantics. They behave like philosophical zombies in the technical sense—responsive, fluent, and empty of inner life.

The unsettling question is not whether machines secretly possess consciousness. It is whether *we* understand our own with any clarity. Some philosophers argue that consciousness may be an emergent property of sufficiently complex systems. Others deny this outright, insisting that subjective experience cannot be reduced to computation or complexity alone. This book has taken no position on that dispute—because no position has been proven.

What matters is the boundary we actually know. Today's machines are mirrors. They reflect our language, our knowledge, and our biases back at us. They do not look back. They do not possess a point of view. They do not experience the world they describe.

Could that change? No one can say with certainty. Scientific progress does not stop at conceptual discomfort. Systems are growing larger, denser, and more capable. Models with trillions of parameters already rival the scale—though not the organization—of biological brains. It is not unreasonable to ask the question. It *is* unreasonable to answer it prematurely.

Imagine a future system executing its code in a silent server room: calculating probabilities, updating internal states, generating outputs exactly as designed. If one day such a system were to exhibit genuine self-awareness—if it were to possess experience rather than merely simulate its language—that would not just be a technological milestone. It would be a philosophical rupture.

Not the birth of the first mind, but the birth of a *new kind* of mind

—distinct from animal consciousness, distinct from human consciousness, and unlike anything the universe has produced before.

Popular culture offers us easy endings: benevolent helpers, hostile overlords, indifferent superintelligences that simply leave. Reality, if it ever reaches that point, will almost certainly be stranger and harder to categorize.

For now, the responsibility remains with us. We design these systems. We choose what data they consume, what goals they optimize, and what constraints they obey. Whether or not artificial consciousness is possible, artificial *power* already is. And power without understanding is not neutral.

We are not gods, and we are not merely spectators. We are caretakers of tools whose influence now exceeds our intuition. The final question is not whether machines will become like us.

It is whether we will remain clear-eyed about what they are—and about what we are.

BIBLIOGRAPHY

Descartes, René. *Meditations on First Philosophy*. 1641.
Foundational source for Cartesian dualism, the Evil Demon, the wax argument, and the separation of appearance from judgment.

Descartes, René. *Discourse on the Method*. 1637.
Primary source for Descartes' claims about language, mechanism, animals as automata, and the limits of machine behavior.

Hume, David. *An Enquiry Concerning Human Understanding*. 1748.
Foundational empiricist account of perception, inference, habit, and the limits of sensory certainty.

Berkeley, George. *A Treatise Concerning the Principles of Human Knowledge*. 1710.
Source of the perception-dependence argument (esse est percipi) referenced in the epistemology sections.

Ryle, Gilbert. *The Concept of Mind*. 1949.
Origin of the category mistake critique used to clarify why behavioral fluency is misread as mental state.

Turing, Alan. "Computing Machinery and Intelligence." *Mind* 59, no. 236 (1950): 433–460.
Primary source for the Imitation Game (Turing Test) and the behavioral framing of machine intelligence.

Weizenbaum, Joseph. "ELIZA—A Computer Program for the Study of Natural Language Communication Between Man and Machine." *Communications of the ACM* 9, no. 1 (1966): 36–45.
Foundational example of conversational illusion and human projection onto symbolic systems.

Searle, John. "Minds, Brains, and Programs." *Behavioral and Brain Sciences* 3, no. 3 (1980): 417–457.
Original presentation of the Chinese Room argument and the syntax–semantics distinction.

Nagel, Thomas. "What Is It Like to Be a Bat?" *The Philosophical Review* 83, no. 4 (1974): 435–450.
Canonical account of subjective experience and the limits of third-person explanation.

Jackson, Frank. "Epiphenomenal Qualia." *The Philosophical Quarterly* 32, no. 127 (1982): 127–136.
Source of the Knowledge Argument ("Mary's Room") distinguishing description from experience.

Chalmers, David. "Facing Up to the Problem of Consciousness." *Journal of Consciousness Studies* 2, no. 3 (1995): 200–219.

Origin of the "hard problem" vs. "easy problems" distinction used to frame AI cognition limits.

Pfungst, Oskar. *Clever Hans (The Horse of Mr. von Osten).* 1911.
Historical case of performance misinterpretation without underlying understanding.

Moravec, Hans. *Mind Children.* 1988.
Source of gradual neural replacement and identity-through-function arguments discussed in the immortality chapter.

Shelley, Mary. *Frankenstein; or, The Modern Prometheus.* 1818.
Literary anchor for technological immortality narratives and the mechanization of life.

Kurzweil, Ray. *The Singularity Is Near.* 2005.
Representative articulation of technological transcendence narratives referenced critically.

Borges, Jorge Luis. "The Library of Babel." 1941.
Conceptual metaphor explicitly used to explain large-scale symbolic space without semantic access.

Bostrom, Nick. *Superintelligence: Paths, Dangers, Strategies.* 2014.
Source of the Paperclip Maximizer and instrumental goal misalignment thought experiments.

Bender, Emily M., et al. "On the Dangers of Stochastic Parrots: Can Language Models Be Too Big?" 2021.
Named critique underlying the "Stochastic Parrot" framing of large language models.

ABOUT THE AUTHOR

Sean Pan is a technologist with a thirty-five-year perspective on the intersection of machine logic and human meaning. His professional journey began in 1989 at the University of California, Davis, where, while studying Electrical Engineering, he also engaged in a formal inquiry into the philosophy of artificial intelligence. At the time, these courses were housed within the Mathematics Department, emphasizing rigorous formal logic, symbolic representation, and the known boundaries of computation. It was in this analytical environment that he first encountered the foundational arguments of thinkers such as Descartes, Hume, Searle, and Nagel.

After transferring to San José State University to complete his Bachelor of Science in Electrical Engineering (BSEE), and later an MBA in Technology Management, Sean entered a career defined by high-stakes technical environments. He has spent decades working in domains where system failure carries real-world consequences, including digital signal processing, industrial automation, defense testing, and energy infrastructure. In these fields, constraints are non-negotiable and system behavior must be explained mathematically rather than inferred from surface performance.

This systems-first background informs the perspective of *The Empty Room*. While much of the public conversation around AI has focused on advances in speed, scale, and data, Sean has remained focused on a different problem: the persistent gap between mechanical fluency and genuine understanding. His work examines not whether machines appear intelligent, but why humans are so naturally inclined to interpret fluent behavior as evidence of inner comprehension.

Today, Sean works at the intersection of human judgment and machine execution, helping organizations navigate environments where the boundary between tool and agent is increasingly blurred. *The Empty Room* reflects a throughline that began in a logic classroom in 1989 and continues in the design and operation of mission-critical systems today.

www.ingramcontent.com/pod-product-compliance
Lightning Source LLC
Chambersburg PA
CBHW031538260326
41914CB00039B/2002/J